T0299257

ROUTLEDGE LIBRARY EDITIONS:
MANAGEMENT

Volume 37

PUBLIC RELATIONS FOR MANAGEMENT SUCCESS

PUBLIC RELATIONS FOR MANAGEMENT SUCCESS

FRANK JEFKINS

LONDON AND NEW YORK

First published in 1984 by Croom Helm Ltd

This edition first published in 2018
by Routledge
4 Park Square, Milton Park, Abingdon, Oxon OX14 4RN
605 Third Avenue, New York, NY 10017

Routledge is an imprint of the Taylor & Francis Group, an informa business

British Library Cataloguing in Publication Data
A catalogue record for this book is available from the British Library

ISBN: 978-1-138-55938-7 (Set)
ISBN: 978-1-351-05538-3 (Set) (ebk)
ISBN: 978-1-138-57162-4 (Volume 37) (hbk)
ISBN: 978-0-203-70261-1 (Volume 37) (ebk)

Public Relations for Management Success

Frank Jefkins

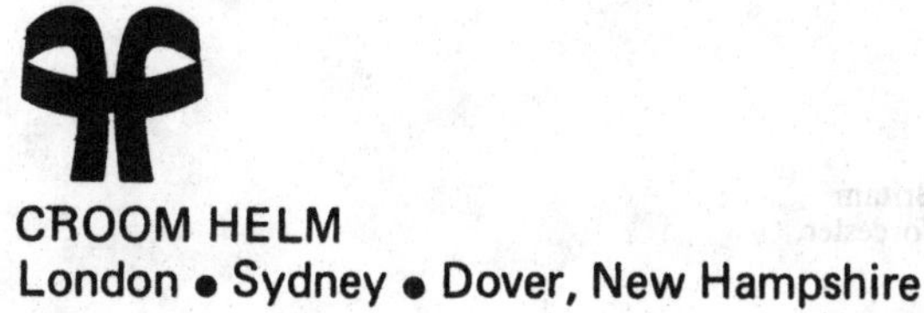

CROOM HELM
London • Sydney • Dover, New Hampshire

Croom Helm Ltd, Provident House, Burrell Row,
Beckenham, Kent BR3 1AT
Croom Helm Australia Pty Ltd, First Floor,
139 King Street, Sydney, NSW 2001, Australia

British Library Cataloguing in Publication Data

Jefkins, Frank
Public relations for management success.
1. Public relations
I. Title
659.2 HM263

ISBN 0-7099-1436-9

Croom Helm, 51 Washington Street,
Dover, New Hampshire, 03820 USA

Library of Congress Cataloging in Publication Data
Main entry under title:

Public relations for management success.

Includes index.
1. Public Relations. 2. Industrial management.
I. Title.
HD59.J43 1984 659.2 84-17669

ISBN 0-7099-1436-9

Printed and bound in Great Britain
by Billing & Sons Limited, Worcester.

CONTENTS

PREFACE

ACKNOWLEDGEMENTS

1.	A Management View of Public Relations	1
2.	Public Relations as an Integral Management Function	5
3.	Tangible Public Relations	14
4.	The Costs of PR	26
5.	Planning a PR Programme	32
6.	Media and Methods	49
7.	Media Relations Techniques	71
8.	Special Action Areas of Modern Public Relations	79
9.	Assessment of Results	106
10.	PR Professionalism	112
11.	Setting up a PR Department	118

Appendix 1: Bibliography 125

Appendix 2: Addresses of Organisations and Services 126

Glossary of Abbreviations 127

Index 129

OTHER BOOKS BY FRANK JEFKINS

Advertising

Advertising Made Simple

Advertising Today

Dictionary of Marketing, Advertising and Public Relations

Effective Marketing Strategy

Effective Press Relations and House Journal Editing

Effective PR Planning

Effective Publicity Writing

Introduction to Marketing, Advertising and Public Relations

Marketing and PR Media Planning

Modern Marketing

Planned Press and Public Relations

Public Relations

Public Relations Made Simple

Public Relations for Marketing Management

DEDICATION

This book was mostly written in Nigeria, Zimbabwe and Malawi where the author was lecturing, and is dedicated to Bankole Akinyemi, Don Lightfoot and Simon Pamdule in each of those countries.

PREFACE

Since 1968 I have been running seminars for PR practitioners in the UK and some 18 countries overseas, plus international Summer Schools since 1980. Everywhere, the common cry has been that management should have attended the courses, and that it is management which needs to learn about public relations.

There seems to be a management attitude of 'why keep a dog and bark yourself' concerning public relations. Yet public relations should start at the top, and the first PRO in a company should be the chief executive officer.

Of course, in the most successful companies, the ones which have survived recession, the growth companies, and many representing the new technologies, this is so.

Generally, however, management can profit from understanding public relations better, and from learning how to use and buy PR services. It should be an essential subject in all management training syllabuses.

Public relations concerns the total communication of any organisation. It is not a form of advertising, nor is it limited to marketing. It is vital to the success of any business.

Significantly, one of the growth businesses in Britain during the 80s is that of the PR consultancies.

Croydon, 1984

ACKNOWLEDGEMENTS

I am grateful to the many sources which have been quoted in this book, and acknowledgements are given in the references at the end of each chapter. My thanks are also due to the many friends and colleagues in the PR profession who were so helpful, often at short notice, in sending me publications, audio-tapes and videos. They include Peter Ambeck-Madsen, Peter Bateman, Christopher Bosanquet, Terence Franklin, Tony Good, Derek Stone and Reginald Watts.

1.

A MANAGEMENT VIEW OF PUBLIC RELATIONS

Communications The Key

Public Relations is seldom any of the things management thinks it is. Try to interest most management in the subject, and they will evade it as something which is handled by someone lower down in the hierarchy. There is a kind of why keep a dog and bark yourself attitude. They either mistrust PR or, worse still, abuse it. Yet the first PRO in any business should be the chief executive officer.

This is because the CEO - or any line manager - will succeed only if he or she is able to communicate. Public relations is the art of communicating in order to obtain understanding through knowledge.

The CEO may head a splendid company with an excellent product or service, but profitability depends on his ability to communicate, and know how to use communicators and their techniques. Thus, ability to communicate should be a primary facet of the job specification of anyone involved in management, no matter at what level.

This requirement extends beyond the elementary need to be articulate and literate. It is not only or even a question of being able to command, advocate or persuade. Business communication is more sophisticated than that. It is necessary to understand what has to be communicated and why, and to whom it is vital to communicate and how. Moreover, communication is an intelligence system, and it is equally important to receive information and gain understanding.

The principle reason for industrial disputes, lost orders, low share prices, take-over threats, unhappy dealerships, staff instability, unsatisfactory exports, slow cash flow and ultimately poor company results lies in management's scepticism or downright ignorance about public relations.

Is this a true assessment of the typical management view of public relations? Generally, yes, although it must be admitted that in our really successful growth companies management does know about PR and there is often a PR director on the board. But this is rare. More often, where it exists at all, PR is relegated to a corner of the marketing department, if the marketing manager admits that such a thing exists. Marketing managers are especially dubious about PR, and it is noticeable that PR is absent from most textbooks on marketing.

Some of the worst offenders are management consultants who rarely know what to do with public relations when recommending the reorganisation of a company, or how to set up a new one. There is much training in business studies and management up to DBA standards, but public relations seldom if ever has an important place in the curriculum. One has only to look at the prospectuses of some of our universities and business schools to find that the subject is ignored and there is not even a visiting lecturer. How, then, are ostensibly trained managers expected to communicate? They may learn something about marketing or advertising, but public relations is evaded.

However, a British MBA programme with a major PR content, is under discussion at the time of writing and could be introduced in 1985.

Part of Management's Job Specification

The answer is probably that if a business manager really wants to manage effectively, and create a rising career for himself, he has to write public relations into his job specification himself. That then entails finding out what PR is all about, applying its principles to his managerial functions, and knowing when and how to augment his own PR efforts with the skills of specialists. But he cannot delegate what he does not understand. It is no use employing a journalist as a sort of guard dog, which is what often happens. A positive commitment to PR is necessary from the top down.

But even when a company is headed by a committed PR-minded CEO, communication problems may occur lower down the organisational tree of command. Misunderstanding of the role of PR often exists within middle-management, among the very people who aspire to top management. Large corporations today have bureaucracies of timid middle-management who are incapable of communicating. Most of them cannot write a letter: they can only pick up a telephone. Preparing a report is like trying to write a will. Taking a decision is like going to the dentist. Does this stem from management training which is all about theories and has forgotten how man first started communicating by drawing pictures on walls?

Visual Communication

It is significant that pictures - video - are rapidly becoming one of the most significant forms of management communication, usually in the hands of the company PRO. Video is often doing the job which management has failed to do. Here is an example.

It happened in one of our twelve regional gas undertakings. The service engineers complained that there was too little work and their earnings were suffering and jobs were at risk. Management told them that when they were carrying out work in customers' homes they should keep their eyes open for customer needs and tell housewives about the new appliances in the showroom. If they could help sales they would get more installation work. The men retorted in true British workman fashion that they were enginers, not salesmen.

The PRO, who produced the video staff magazine, heard about this. He set up an interview with the trade union official and asked him whether it would not be a good idea if service engineers encouraged their customers to visit the showroom to see the new cookers and refrigerators. Splendid idea, agreed the trade union official. The interview went out to 90 locations in the next edition of the video magazine. The CEO couldn't believe it - but why hadn't he communicated so subtly in the first place? You have to negotiate from a position of strength, in this case having the trade union on your side. The men took the advice of their union official and so boosted their earning capacity.

A CEO's Attitude to Communication

The Chairman of one of our international growth companies - whose share price always makes good reading in the city prices - once scared his middle management by saying 'Tell them everything - we're bound to do 50 per cent of the business.' Middle management always seems to have an in-built fear of industrial espionage. Trade secrets are often a myth invented by the uncourageous. This same chairman also told his PRO that he should know more about the company than anyone else in it. When a director wanted the PRO fired for refusing to have his photograph taken for largely reasons of vanity, the Chairman said the PRO was in a special position and if he decided 'no pictures' there would be no pictures.

When that PRO moved on to better his career, the Chairman sent him a thank you note saying 'our PR is the envy of our competitors.' Here was a CEO who knew what PR was all about, and what he wanted from PR. The company spent little on advertising, but with the Chairman's inspiration the entire staff were involved in PR. Such is the reputation of that company that 60 per cent of its business is said to come from recommendations. When it went public some years ago - in spite of a depressed stock market - its shares were heavily over-subscribed, and there have since been two scrip issues on top of high dividends.

Those Favourable Images!

The knack of being a good communicator lies in frankness and appreciation of the fact that the real world is full of good and bad days, successes and failures, profits and losses. The mistaken idea is that public relations is about favourable images, favourable climates of opinion, favourable this and that. It would be very nice if that were true. Public relations is about facts, about the real, hard world in which it may be enough to be fully and properly understood, let alone loved. One day the product is a brand leader, next day the bottom has fallen out of the market.

Management which understands PR is able to deal with all situations. It does not expect PR to act as a smoke-screen, a trouble-shooter, a pretender that bad things never happen. Today in some of our more sensitive disaster-prone industries, wise management has introduced crisis management with the PRO organised in advance to deal with serious situations. This is management aware of the need to communicate quickly, accurately and effectively so that the company is not placed at the mercy of media rumour-mongering and speculation.

The same thing applies to that major growth area of PR - management-employee communications. With PR-orientated management, the grapevine is uprooted and the 'teatime' strikes do not occur. Greater worker participation has to be management inspired so that employees know why it would be stupid to kill the cow which produces the milk. An organisation which has grown in membership and influence in recent years is the International Association of Business Communicators which aims to develop the house journal editor into a more wide-ranging internal business communicator. Management can benefit from supporting the role of the internal PRO.

Perhaps it is significant that in Britain, in spite of recession, the PR consultancy world has found the 80s their most profitable. Partly it has been because advertising has been found to be less cost-effective than was previously believed, but mainly it has been because more wide-awake management has recognised the need to communicate so much to so many publics. Industries have changed, new technologies have emerged, and businesses survive only so long as they are known, understood and respected, not just by customers but by all those who influence survival from politicians to investment analysts, employees to media pundits.

2.
PUBLIC RELATIONS AS AN INTEGRAL MANAGEMENT FUNCTION

Introduction

In the previous chapter public relations was defined quite simply as creating understanding through knowledge, and while this concerns the total communications of the whole organisation with all its publics, it stops at understanding. Beyond this point other more persuasive forms of communication proceed into the realms of marketing, salesmanship, advertising and sales promotion. In other non-commercial organisations such as government, political parties, trade unions and religious denominations, persuasive communications become progaganda.

Public relations, far-embracing although it is, stops at understanding for a very practical reason. It has to be credible. Public relations fails if it exceeds this limit and indulges in bias which is acceptable in persuasive, promotional or propagandist communication.

This need to be impartial often baffles people engaged in management, marketing and advertising. But the simple fact is that PR's strength lies in its acceptance by all the recipients of PR information, including the media.

At the same time, the persuasive activities do have their PR element in that PR is about goodwill and reputation stemming from good behaviour. A business will be judged by its behaviour, and if it adopts malpractices such as over-charging, dubious selling methods, poor products, late delivery or offensive or misleading advertising, this will detract from its good name. Thus, PR will seek to create understanding that a business is deserving of its good name.

Bernard Levin once accused PR of pretending that things were what they were not. Such falsifications may be the aim of some misguided management, but that is as much a malpractice, and an abuse of PR, as selling medicines which cannot possibly alleviate let alone cure. Credible PR is a powerful stimulant of good business; its abuse is silly.

Unfortunately, management is not encouraged to understand the proper and valuable use of PR when it is so often misrepresented by the media. Two examples of this are when the media refer to public relations practitioners as 'hidden persuaders', borrowing that misleading expression from Vance Packard's[1] excellent book of that name which was about an entirely different subject, namely motivational research. Again, whenever a government conducts a policy which is regarded with suspicion by the media (such as an arms reduction proposal) the media calls it 'merely a PR exercise' when it has nothing remotely to do with PR. Management, frequently faced by sceptical references to PR, is therefore inclined to either shy away from PR - or mis-use it as they believe they are expected to do.

There are also distinct differences between North American and European attitudes towards public relations, some of which have been imported into Britain by the big American PR consultancies which dominate British consultancy practice. In North America, marketing, salesmanship and advertising are more acceptable ways of life than they are in Britain. Consequently, American PR tends to be more promotional than its British counterpart. In Britain, the media dislike anything smacking of advertising. To be credible, to be acceptable, and to make PR work in Britain it is essential that it be confined to the creation of mutual understanding and leaves partial, promotional, persuasive communication to the worlds of advertising and propaganda. This is a sensible division because PR has quite sufficient to do in seeking to create understanding. It is not pious but practical policy to keep persuasion out of the PR business. Public relations aims to inform and educate while advertising aims to persuade and sell. Both may be necessary but PR will not work if it persuades, and advertising will not work if it fails to persuade.

All this perversion of public relations is not helped by the weevil in management's very midst. Marketing has become a vital part of many businesses. But marketing people are often very misinformed about PR, and this weakness is often transmitted to higher management. We must also include marketers as part of the management structure. Immediately, we have an important part of the management structure which is poisoned by its ignorance of or abuse of PR. Why is this?

One reason, put to the author by marketing lecturers, was that marketing itself was having to struggle for acceptance, and this led them to be sceptical of public relations which they felt was even less acceptable than marketing! Public relations people are not so professionally inhibited, and they take their profession seriously. The problem with those marketing lecturers was that they were teaching the wrong kind of marketing, largely because they relied on out-dated American texts. In the 80s employers were finding that marketing graduates were out-of-touch with modern marketing.

Marketing Attitudes to Public Relations

Marketing, as distinct from selling, was imported from the USA. It became so important in Britain that the former Institute of Sales Management was renamed the Institute of Marketing. Publishing houses which used to employ 'space salesman' now employ 'marketing executives'. In recent years, building societies have set up marketing departments to sell investments. Put simply, instead of selling what has been produced, a business now produces what it can sell. Market research is used to find out what the market will buy.

Students of marketing are very largely taught from American texts, the most famous being those of Philip Kotler. Not surprisingly notions about PR adopted by marketing students and marketing management are those expressed (if at all) by American writers on marketing. These notions are so distorted that marketing students, teachers, other writers on the subject and those who practice marketing, all over the world, are sceptical about PR. They tend to regard it as a black art which they may well use if it suits their purpose.

In Britain, one has only to attend the annual conference of the Marketing Education Group (representing marketing teachers) to appreciate how poorly they regard PR. It is possible at such a conference for no-one to even mention PR, as if it was a forbidden topic.

Again, this is understandable if we look at the works of Philip Kotler, and his peculiar definition of 'publicity'[2] (Kotler's misinterpretation of public relations) proves the point. He defines publicity (that is, public relations) as:

> *'non-personal stimulation of demand for a product, service or business unit by planting commercially significant news about it in a published medium or obtaining favourable presentation of it upon radio, television, or stage that is not paid for by the sponsor.'*

It will be explained in later chapters that the business news story is not 'planted', favourable presentation may be impossible and accurate or factual presentation may be more to the point, and even press relations cost money to conduct.

A More Realistic Definition

To relish the silliness of the above we have only to consider The Mexican Statement which was produced at the international conference of PR institutes held in Mexico City in August 1978.

> *Public relations practice is the art and science of analysing trends, predicting their consequences, counselling organisation leaders, and implementing planned programmes of action which will serve both the 'organisations' and the public interest.*

What a contrast! The Mexican Statement is a definition which management can understand, get to grips with and apply. For instance, it guides management's thinking on how to practice, employ and, if necessary, buy PR in the form of an in-house PRO or external PR consultant. It is not just or even at all about getting favourable messages published by the media. Public relations is looked at in long-term programme form. Before any advice can be given or any action can be taken research is necessary to find out the extent of or lack of understanding that exists about a business.

What conceptions or misconceptions are held by those with whom management has to communicate, either all of the time or part of the time? Only foolish management ignores opinions and attitudes, for communication is a dialogue. Wars begin through lack of communication, which finally has to take place at the peace table. Today, management has to communicate at all levels, inside and outside the business, otherwise there are industrial disputes, resistance by distributors, and lack of confidence among customers. But first it must 'appreciate the situation', which is sometimes called the 'communication audit'.

As Reginald Watts[3], chairman of Burson-Marsteller the PR consultants has said, management does not always understand what people think of their business. Sometimes they do not even know what their own employees think of the business which employs them. To quote Reginald Watts:

> 'I think it is one of the great fallacies that the directors of companies really understand how the company is seen... certainly the work we have done in this whole field has shown that the senior management of a company are the least informed as to how that company is seen by its outside audiences... the advantage of the (communication) audit is that a company which has not really developed any major public relations activity in the past .... is a little nervous about it .... is enabled to take the first step into public relations'.

Once opinions and attitudes, and the corporate image, are known their consequences can be studied and predicted, and advice can be sought or given, or at least management can take direct heed of the revelations. Employees may have a totally false idea of the company's profitability, or what it does with its profits, or about its prospects. There may be critics who think the company is involved in all sorts of undesirable practices. Customers may be unconvinced about the company's policies. The stock market may be wary of the company's financial standing. There could be resentment among distributors. Management may adopt a dictatorial attitude and say these matters are no-one else's business, but more than likely management may have no knowledge of perilous situations. Strikes may be imminent, pressure groups may be assembling damaging cases, customers may be transferring their loyalties, and a take-over might be brewing. A foreign importer may be about to steal their trade.

But communicated wisdom can lead to the planning of PR programmes to avert disasters, assuming that they can be averted if the true facts are made known or wrongs can be righted and also made known. This is where professional public relations techniques can be applied provided, as the Mexican Statement says, this can be done responsibly in everyone's interest. Crisis PR will be examined more closely in Chapter 8.

Let us look at this retrospectively. In the past, a number of companies have suffered business disasters. Were they unavoidable? In all cases the marketing operation was planned and supported by management, and it was done without any thought for the PR consequences.

Some Marketing Failures

For years, one of the world's largest motor-car manufacturers, General Motors, regarded 'safety' as a negative selling proposition, and it took an intensive consumerist campaign to get motor-cars designed with safety as a positive selling proposition. Today, safety is a major selling factor adopted by the best motor-car manufacturers. German motor-car manufacturers in particular have for the past twenty years made a major selling point of the ability of the front and rear ends of their vehicles to crush on impact, leaving the passenger section rigid. 'Programmed deformation' has become an internationally accepted selling factor in motor-car marketing.

The first non-drip one-coat paint was advertised as if its apparently novel qualities would produce an immediate response. Paint dealers stocked up, and stockists were listed in press advertisements. The campaign broke at Easter with excellent timing for a do-it-yourself home decorating product. The marketing strategy was excellent. But it failed to sell the new paint because PR had been ignored. Impressed by the advertising, would-be customers went to the listed shops. The men behind those counters are experts who can advise their customers. When asked about the new paint they scorned it. They had been trained to apply under-coats and top coats, so they derided the unorthodox product. As a result, the customers bought a standard brand, and the new product sat unsold on the shelves.

The manufacturer had to turn to PR to educate the retailer. It took about 18 months of sustained PR effort. Then sales took off, the main competitor had to produce a similar product, and today Magicote is a best-seller.

When Thoresen first introduced drive-on drive-off car ferries to Britain, and a new Southampton-Cherbourg route, it was a marketing failure. It was taken up by the motoring organisations only (AA and RAC), and ignored by the myriads of travel agencies. Like the paint retailers, travel agents advise their customers. Who ever travelled to France via Southampton? People had been crossing the Channel by the shortest sea route since 1066! Consequently, Thoresen had to resort to an intensive PR campaign to educate travel agents before the next season's bookings began. A Viking ferry did a round Britain tour, with travel agents from inland towns being taken to ports where the ferry was berthed. Next season, Britain's travel agents knew all about Thoresen services. They understood what a drive-on drive-off ferry was like and the route taken by Thoresen.

This is a good example of the PR power of understanding rather than the advertising power of persuasion. As with the Magicote example above you cannot persuade people who do not understand.

For decades, many tasty breakfast cereals were sold in vast quantities, but their food value was probably only the added milk and sugar. Authorities in the USA insisted that these products should include added food values. Today these popular products are promoted on the basis of the additives.

Not long ago cigarette manufacturers introduced 'safe' cigarettes made of New Smoking Mixture instead of tobacco. Fortunes were spent on massive advertising campaigns. It was argued that the product was bound to sell since 50 per cent of the people were anti-smoking. The fortunes were lost and, save for one or two minority brands, the product has disappeared. Stocks had to be withdrawn from the shops and destroyed. Why? Because the non-smokers did not buy the 'safe' cigarette, and regular smokers preferred to smoke real cigarettes however lethal. The marketing people had failed to realise that the smokers needed to be educated so that they would welcome the product when it was eventually launched. Blunderbus advertising tactics can be costly.

Numerous products are nowadays banned under the British Code of Advertising Practice, and the IBA Code of Practice, and controlled by scores of laws to mention only the Trade Descriptions Acts. Why is all this voluntary or self-regulatory and legal consumer protection necessary? Why was Ralph Nader necessary? Because companies, including some very 'respectable' ones, did not or still do not do their PR homework. Marketing departments have been and are still permitted to foist undesirable products on consumers, or to use undesirable promotional tactics. All these malpractices rebound on their perpetrators, and that is bad PR. This may be the 'unacceptable face of capitalism' based on caveat emptor, but is it necessary or is it merely an example of the American marketing ideal of maximising profits going too far?

In all the examples given above, top management was at fault, and in many cases it was ill-advised by its marketing management which had failed to understand the PR implications of its blundering activities. A great deal of business failure is due to the fact that public relations are dirty words to marketers, whereas PR should be inherent in the total marketing strategy, and an essential part of the marketing manager's everyday thinking.

Instead, marketers think in Kotlerian terms, regarding PR as part of the promotion mix and free advertising or publicity at best. The frightening thing is that marketing schools, and not only in Britain, are wedded to teaching the Kotler concept, which is disastrous from a management point of view. It is in total conflict with the realities that concern top management daily. The narrow Kotlerian view of PR as mere 'publicity' is nonsense as any CEO knows if he is a capable communicator.

PR Versus Free Advertising

Let us kill the myth of free advertising. Few things are free in this world, except fresh air and the elements. Public relations and advertising are two different things. The only reason why any responsible editor or radio/TV producer will use PR material is because it is likely to be of sufficient reader or audience interest to merit being used. This in turn will help to either maintain or increase readership or audience figures.

Taken to the extreme, it will help the editor or producer to keep his job.

It is only in advertising features (produced independently of the editorial), or in very small circulation journals, that editorial material will be published to please advertisers or as an inducement to advertise. Generally, editors and producers are unsympathetic towards advertising. In fact, many newspapers and magazines are no longer subsidised by advertising (because of the rise in production costs), and high cover prices are relied upon for revenue.

A PR story for the media must therefore seek publication on its merits as news, whether in the 'hard news' columns or in the special interest features. Any form of 'puffery' will cause the story to be rejected. Yet it is not uncommon for management to believe that they have a right to be published, forgetting that the commercial media are businesses just like their own. The British press does not even enjoy quite the constitutional status of the Fourth Estate, as in the USA, although the expression is used in Britain. The criteria of all material supplied to the media must, in the first place, be whether it is of interest and value to the reader, viewer and listener, NOT the sender. If it is used the sender gets his reward, but to achieve that reward it must be the secondary consideration.

To management this may seem absurd. They are not working for the media! But neither should management seek to exploit the media. If they want the support of the media they must also support them, which is known as servicing the media. Understanding the nature of publishing and broadcasting is another important facet of public relations.

So, while there is no point in trying to get blatant advertising into the media nor is accepted material free advertising. The report will be factual and without comment, other than the editor's. There will be no advocacy, only a statement of facts, and without persuasion it cannot be advertising. It will be publicity but - to contradict the Kotler version of that word - publicity can be good or bad, and anything which is made known publicly is publicised. Some people seek to avoid publicity.

Again, PR coverage cannot be assessed in advertising terms, although this yardstick is sometimes used and the Americans like this form of evaluation. The method of saying so much space or airtime is worth so much in advertising terms is nonsense. In the first place, editorial space or programme time is priceless, and in the second it is unlikely that similar space or airtime would ever be purchased for advertising purposes. A sponsored golf tournament might occupy hours of television viewing time, with frequent reminders of the sponsor's name, but to buy such a volume of air time would be formidable.

The Image

Few words have caused more misunderstanding about PR than the word image. It is a word the PR profession would like to forget. It has led to management seeking 'favourable' images, and to the advertising and journalism fraternity talking glibly of 'polishing tarnished images'. Both are contradictions of what an image really is and since this book is about public relations for business success let us confine ourselves to the corporate image.

The corporate image is the impression various people have of the business organisation. It is sometimes called the perceived image, meaning the impression people have as a result of their knowledge and experience of the organisation. Obviously, this will vary from person to person. Images change or grow as knowledge varies or increases. A European may have an image of Africa as a country rather than a continent, where black people live, and be surprised to learn that there are fifty African countries populated by very different Africans. India has long retained its false image of the Taj Mahal and elephants by those who do not know it is one of the ten largest industrial countries in the world. One has only to travel abroad to discover how trivial were one's home-based images of foreign places. Understanding stems from knowledge, and, as we have already said, that is what public relations is all about.

It is the responsibility of management to care about the perceived image of the business, not to perpetuate some paternal mirror image or invent a wish image. Awareness of the external current image is vital. Does it match up to the truth, and is the truth a worthy one? There is no point in hiring an image maker, like they do in politics to 'make' a president or a prime minister as if a person can be sold like a can of beans. It is interesting that advertising agencies, not PR consultants, are hired to 'make' politicians. The Saatchi's and Saatchi's are not PR practitioners, as we have seen with the abuse of communications during recent elections when even the Advertising Standards Authority was powerless to take action.

A business will perform most easily and successfully when its image is based on sound knowledge of its policies, abilities and prospects. Management which is efficient, proud and frank has a good story to tell which will produce its own well-deserved image. The company which makes reliable goods, maintains good after-sales service, has a record of good industrial relations, has excellent trade relations and is socially responsible, finds its reward in industrial peace, successful sales, high profits and strong share prices. Its enviable corporate image is assured, provided people are aware of these things. The best public relations programmes are those which concentrate on regularly having a good story to tell.

It is not always true that the media believe that bad news is good news. William Randolph Hearst was wrong when he said 'news is what people don't want you to print, the rest is advertising.' The press print plenty of good news about businesses they respect such as Marks and Spencer (who do not advertise), BL since they improved their product and made a profit, British Airways since they made a profit, and geniuses like Sinclair who can beat the Japanese at their own game.

Management must be responsible for seeing that a business has the image it desires. They must not be reluctant heroes, like the management of Courtaulds years ago which forgot to tell people how good it was and was nearly taken over by ICI. In such ways public relations becomes an integral management function, at all management levels. The CEO should be a company's ambassador, not its secret service chief.

There has been a progressive change in the nature of business leadership. From the entrepreneur top management moved to accountants, and then to marketers, and now we are finding a number of former PROs becoming CEOs. We even find people who are being groomed for high office having to spend a spell as PRO. But were there ever such good PROs as the succeeding heads of Marks and Spencer? The image of Marks and Spencer is probably the most consistent in all British business.

Integrating PR With Management

From the foregoing discussion about the nature and role of public relations in business three things emerge:

First, PR - communication to create understanding through knowledge - enters into every manager's job specification.

Second, managers at all levels need to work closely with and make the greatest possible use of their in-house PRO or outside PR consultant, who cannot work well in isolation.

Third, managers (and especially top management) must know what they want from their PR advisers, and that entails knowing how to buy PR services. On the one hand, management should be PR-minded and on the other be aware of and know how to employ specialists. Ideally, the PR practitioner should report to the CEO and co-operate with all other departments such as production, finance, personnel and marketing. As quoted in Chapter One, the CEO should expect his PRO to know more about the company than anyone else in it. In an efficient company the PRO will be a board director and the PR adviser to the board.

REFERENCES

1. Packard, Vance, *The Hidden Persuaders*, Penguin, London, 1957.
2. Kotler, Philip, *Marketing Management*, 3rd Ed, Prentice-Hall, London, 1976.
3. Watts, Reginald, *The Communications Audit*, a taped interview with Derek Bloom, Burson-Marsteller Ltd., 1982.

3.

TANGIBLE PUBLIC RELATIONS

A favourite myth about public relations is that it is intangible and its results cannot be evaluated. If management has that idea about PR it is no wonder they are sceptical about it. Management wants results. Why spend money on something illusionary? This is where those useless expressions about favourable images and favourable climates of opinion are so vague and misleading. Some organisations can never expect to be regarded favourably, or at least not all of the time. Public relations has to deal with the realities of a world which is a mixture of good and bad, ups and downs, not only with the good and ups as if the opposite never occur.

For instance, most public service companies have to deal with the majority of the general public. How can you ever please them all? It is very difficult for the post office, the telephone company or the water, gas or electricity undertaking to enjoy a constantly favourable relationship with all their customers all of the time. Every public service utility or enterprise uses PR extensively to explain what is going on. It is important that customers understand why services are delayed, accidents have occurred, and prices have been increased; why there is an industrial dispute, and how the introduction of new technologies will effect customers. They may not like any of these things, but they are kept informed and that knowledge can have the tangible effect of reducing complaints and obtaining the co-operation of customers.

Nothing creates more antagonism than ignorance about why something has gone wrong. Why has the flight been delayed, why is there a power failure, why is the mail late, why are there so few policemen on the beat? The answer may not be very favourable to the giver, but it often achieves a degree of satisfaction that is in itself an expression of goodwill.

Management By Objectives Approach

The secret of tangible PR is that if you have objectives you can measure or actually see the results. There is no point in spending money on PR just to have the pleasure of admiring a collection of press cuttings. Press cuttings are history. What matters is what did those press stories achieve? Or the house journal, the documentary film, the TV interview, the seminar, the exhibition or whatever the chosen medium. Too many PR campaigns stop at just producing something, especially the bill.

In Chapter Five we shall consider planning objective PR programmes, using the well-known Six Point PR Planning Model, but here let us anticipate the full plan by examining a large number of potential tangible objectives under specific headings. For budgeting reasons, the full PR prgoramme will be based on a certain number of objectives such as the following:

1. Recruitment

Recession and unemployment has not made recruitment of staff unnecessary. Recruitment requires two things, attracting the right calibre of applicants, and convincing the right applicants that you are a desirable employer. The PR objective is thus to reach such potential employees wherever they may be in colleges, universities, in other employment, locally, nationally or even internationally. How this is done calls for PR techniques, but Michelin did it very well by placing advertisements which offered a tape recording to graduates. The audio-cassette tape recording described the company and its opportunities for graduates, suitably dramatised with sound effects such as those of Grand Prix motor racing.

Recruitment is not only about advertising vacancies or commissioning head hunters. There can be handicaps such as the location of the company, the nature of its business, its national origin, its involvement in some controversy, its industrial relations record or maybe its disappointing financial performance. Those negative states of hostility, prejudice, apathy or ignorance may operate against it being a desirable employer. The overall PR programme to establish a correct corporate image and understanding will, of course, contribute in a general sense to successful recruitment. Just as premature advertising (as we have already seen) can fail through lack of preliminary PR, so recruitment advertising can fail if job-seekers have inhibitions about the job advertiser.

It may be that while recruitment is a specific objective it can be absorbed in the total programme, but it is more likely that as potential employees form an isolated public some special PR activities directed at sources of recruits or at the recruits themselves will have to be devised.

Special efforts may therefore be necessary. Many of our leading companies make a regular practice of participating in careers evenings at schools, distributing documentary films to schools, or inviting sixth-formers to attend weekend courses at company training centres.

2. Internal Relations

The trend towards more open management, more worker participation - long established in countries like Germany and Holland and advocated in the UK by the Liberals and the SDP - and a move away from the class-ridden British master-and-man attitude, is encouraging increasing attention to internal relations. The 'English disease' of industrial disruption is not only the fault of craft rather than industrial unions, our public school traditions, or lack of works council and worker directors. It is basically a PR problem of poor upward and downward communication. The PR objective here is to improve (or even establish!) management-employee relations.

The answer is not to provide a sports field, an annual outing, and a free but paternal house journal. A dialogue is needed. Even familiarity with who is who is needed.

The CEO of one international company had the right idea. He said to his managers: what do you want a secretary for? Get out from behind your desk and go round the branches. Everyone in that company knew who was managing. They did it on their feet, not with office memos. Even in recession that company hits the financial headlines. It has a person-to-person management which has people selling, starting with the girl on the telephone when a potential customer makes an enquiry.

Today, thanks to new information technology, it is becoming increasingly easy to achieve this objective. Downward communication is achieved by video in explaining the annual report and accounts or through managerial interviews in video magazines. Upward communication is achieved by correspondence in house hournals, 'Speak up' suggestion schemes, incentive schemes, and video magazine interviews with employees which show a lot of managers what the staff actually do. That last point is important: how many CEOs and line managers actually know what people do in their companies? All these revelations create people relations and, after all, public relations is really human relations. A lot of industrial disputes occur simply because neither management nor employees know what the other does. Too many businesses are industrial ant hills of mutually hostile people.

The internal communications audit is an excellent and revealing way of appreciating the internal situation before deciding on a particular programme. This kind of study is conducted by an independent unit (such as a PR consultancy which specialises in this work), and an investigator will conduct confidential interviews at all levels of the company to discover the communication strengths, weaknesses and needs. After a study which may take several weeks or even two or three months in complex organisations, a report and recommendation will be produced. To overcome the reluctance of people to be frank, absolute confidentiality must be guaranteed, and the investigator must have access to everyone.

The resultant report can be devastating and certainly enlightening. All sorts of managerial assumptions about loyalty or disinterest, stability or absenteeism, may be shattered for management really has little idea what employees think, believe and want beyond a pay packet. This may seem very strange when one considers the cost of labour, even in days of robots and computers, and the proportion of price which is consumed by this cost. And it is not just a case of labour relations but also management relations.

A survey was conducted some years ago to discover employee attitudes to profits, starting out with the assumption that workers would have a socialistic opposition to profits. On the contrary, workers interviewed believed in profits, but to a man they were convinced that companies made far bigger profits than they actually did. A company may make millions but they may represent a small percentage of the turnover. And what happens to those profits may be mis-understood for, again, only a small percentage will go to shareholders. Misconceptions such as these contribute to industrial disputes. The video version of the balance sheet, using TV personality Michael Barratt as done for some years by Ocean Transport and Trading, and shown to staff world-wide in a matter of days, is excellent internal PR.

More candid management, more freedom for self-expression, can go a long way towards obviating the 'industrial mole' situation which occurred at BL in 1983. Most industrial action is bred on fear, mistrust, ignorance and quite plainly lack of information which should be freely available.

Under the heading of Internal Relations there are special areas which could be selected as individual PR objectives, these being:

(a) To maintain stability. It costs a lot of money to recruit staff, and this is wasted if they leave. Why do they leave? If it is because they are discontented, or other employers are able to tempt them, solutions must be found. Part of PR is putting wrong things right, not pretending faults do not exist. A programme to reverse instability can be to discover the cause or causes and eradicate them. It could be bad management at some level! In one case it was intolerable levels which made it impossible for employees to communicate with one another.

(b) To increase awareness of company policy. Better understanding on this score could help to increase productivity through confidence. Employees who believe in a company are sure of their job security, and there is nothing like enthusiasm for overcoming apathy, absenteeism and poor production figures. We have seen this at various times in the coal industry.

(c) To improve safety standards. Accidents can occur through carelessness such as running on hard shiny floors, bad driving, failure to wear safety helmets or goggles, not using safety devices and so on. Again, it is a communication problem and lack of understanding.

(d) To encourage employees to take up share offers. Having a stake in the company one works for can increase interest, pride and anxiety about its progress. Profit-sharing schemes are good, but there is no commitment like owning a part of the business.

(e) To integrate the staff when there are mergers and acquisitions. Delicate situations arise in these circumstances. There can be fears and jealousies between the staff of the original company and those of the one acquired, especially if they were once rivals. Some organisations go through a series of amalgamations, and there can be constant risk of friction if a programme of unifying PR activities is not conducted. The motor-car and hotel industries are prime examples of this amalgamation process.

(f) To make known promotion prospects within the firm. If this is company policy, as it is in Marks and Spencer, these opportunities need to be well publicised from the induction and training period onwards. It may be a case of regularly reporting the progress being made by members of the staff, which may not be obvious if the company has many branches or locations.

Tangible Public Relations

All the above examples are PR objectives which can have tangible, visible results. They indicate the big difference between planned, objective internal relations, and the cosy, paternal sort of employee relations programmes which aim merely to create a better management-employee atmosphere or relationship, relying chiefly on management providing free services rather than involving the staff in the fortunes of the company in their own interests.

3. Community Relations

It is often said that public relations begin on the doorstep with good neighbour relations. Some businesses have unpleasant characteristics such as smoke, fumes, smells, noise, dust, dirt or effluent which pollute the environment. This may be inevitable or it may be controllable. Even a farm, seemingly pleasant enough, can exude smells of manure, or dangerous smoke when stubble is burned. An airport has difficulty in avoiding noise, and so night flights have to be banned. The extent to which a company will avoid distressing its neighbours is an exercise in public relations.

There can be many objectives in seeking good community relations. Some of these objectives may be:

(a) To attract staff.

(b) To earn the assistance of local government when required.

(c) To prevent vandalism.

(d) To maintain the support of the local MP.

(e) To avoid criticism in the media.

(f) To be associated with the good name of the town like Rowntrees of York, Harveys of Bristol or Boots of Nottingham.

(g) To show company staff that their employer contributes to their community.

Participation in local affairs or consideration for local interests are important management responsibilities calling for truly good relations with the local community. Management awareness of community relations should be voluntary, not sought after. A PR-minded CEO will ask himself how his company can contribute as a member of the community. He needs to keep in touch with what is going on.

4. Financial Relations

A major development in recent decades has been specialist financial public relations, and in London alone there are some thirty PR consultancies which concentrate on this field. Management of public companies which neglect their PR are acting foolishly because misunderstandings in the City could be disastrous. Typical financial PR objectives may be:

(a) To support a new share issue. This can occur when a private company goes public, a nationalised industry is privatised or an existing quoted company seeks to raise funds by a new share issue or debenture. The best support is derived from the accumulative effort of good PR in the past. To be successful, a new share needs to be taken up by the

institutions, such as banks, insurance companies, pension funds and unit trusts which frequently buy large blocks of shares. This calls for confidence based on knowledge of the company's history, management, policy and prospects. The prospects alone will not provide this confidence.

The sale of shares in the privatised Cable and Wireless was highly successful, in spite of the fact that the company's activities were scattered abroad in more than 70 countries, because of the City's high regard for the company. Even so, it is much easier to sell the shares of a company such as BP which is a household name, whose 1983 issue was over-subscribed six times. Years of good PR work made it possible for Rentokil shares to be handsomely over-subscribed when it went public some years ago, in spite of the disadvantage that there was no similar company on the market and it was difficult to set a premium. A striking price was possible for BP since there were already BP shares on the market.

But even a good reputation may not sell shares as was seen by the failure of the Government's attempt to sell off more Cable and Wireless shares in December 1983. Only 70 per cent of the 100 million shares were sold at the minimum tender price of 275p instead of the expected striking price of 300p. The underwriting bankers Kleinwort Benson were left to pay £82.5 million. Why? Probably not so much over worries about C & W's Hong Kong and China ventures as stock market resistance to the greed of the Government's overall privatisation programme, the C & W offer being sandwiched between the huge BP success mentioned above and the impending sale of British Telecom stock.

(b) To maintain the share price. A share price cannot be maintained at a steady price artificially. But if the company has a commendable story to tell in corporate and financial terms, this consistantly good news will help to prevent fluctuations or drastic falls. This is not easy to achieve because the share market (as the FT index indicates) is a temperamental barometer affected by all kinds of extraneous influences including, say, the value of the pound abroad, American interest rates or a foreign war or insurrection over which the PRO or PR consultant has no control. Nevertheless, it is interesting - if one studies the stock market figures - that some company prices move up and down only a point or two and perhaps tend to rise while others (like oil companies) are more volatile. The interim and final dividends are, of course, other indicators.

(c) To avoid a take-over. This can be coupled with the previous objective. A low or falling share price could encourage a take-over bid. When Spillers gave up plant baking following strikes and wage increases which made it unprofitable to meet the competitive demands of the supermarkets, its turnover, profits and share price dropped so that it became victim to a successful bid by Dalgety. This was in spite of a courageous PR effort by Spillers, but it was too late and Spillers were in too weak a position to beat off the Dalgety bid.

(d) To inform city editors, brokers and investment analysts. Financial PR must not be over-done, otherwise suspicions can be invited, but a PR programme can be conducted to make sure that those responsible for giving opinions or advice know what they are talking

about.The City has been described as 'a village' and as such it is a gossip shop. Investment analysts prepare detailed reports on companies as investment prospects, and these influential reports can be damaging if the facts are incorrect. It is important, therefore, that compilers of such reports are kept well informed.

Here we have yet another instance of the danger of persuasion and the need for PR to be important. A few years ago some New York PR consultancies boosted the value of American securities only to disappoint buyers when trading results failed to reach expectations. These consultants were strongly criticised by Wall Street for persuading the stock market to buy the shares on the basis of biased information.

(e) To announce company results and conduct AGMs. The company report has gone through two stages, one good and one bad. Some have been too ornate with fancy print and colour pictures. Others have been produced in such a clear and simplified form that they have been intelligible to people with no special knowledge of accountancy. The production of the annual report and accounts has become a skilled PR task. However, some companies still make the mistake of thinking that the annual report is the start and finish of financial PR. The AGM itself has taken on many new techniques such as video presentations, teleconferencing and phone-ins to enhance communication facilities for interested shareholders.

(f) To inform individual shareholders. The institutional shareholders may be significant, but the small investor with a modest portfolio, perhaps depending on his or her bank manager - or simply the city page - for advice must not be neglected. As William P. Dunk and G.A. Kraut, the New York financial PR consultants have said[1] 'Win support of the individual investor. He adds loyalty and liquidity to your shareholder base. And he's one hedge against unfriendly take-overs.' Two for one scrip issues encourage stability of share-holding (Rentokil have done this twice in a comparatively short time, and on each occasion seen their share price climb again), but it helps if small shareholders read about their investment, or are advised by their bank manager not to sell their shares. Even the popular press carries financial news these days.

(g) To inform overseas stock markets. Many shares are nowadays sold on exchanges and bourses world-wide, particularly in Europe and Asia where there are similar outlets for information through the financial press and investment analysts. Newspapers such as the *International Herald Tribune* and the European edition of the *Wall Street Journal* are useful media, while the *Financial Times* has an international circulation as do magazines such as *The Economist.*

Financial relations should therefore be a form of PR that management should readily understand, appreciate and engage in.

Other Financial Houses

While this section has concentrated on the share market it should not be forgotten that the financial world extends far beyond the stock exchange. Millions of people invest in other forms of security and use a variety of financial services. These include banks, insurance companies, friendly societies and building societies. All of these could have lists of objectives set out for them. Mainly, they are concerned with gaining understanding of the benefits they have to offer.

In these businesses we have seen tremendous competition, especially between banks and building societies. But whereas the banks are old hands at PR, and are larger units more capable of conducting nationwide PR, the building societies (in spite of amalgamations) are still very numerous and they are often fairly regional. They have come to adopt PR more recently. Some building societies have tended to concentrate overmuch on marketing tactics such as expensive television advertising. This can have an adverse effect since investors are apt to suspect that their money is being spent on advertising which keeps their interest down or their charges up. Since building societies occupy prime sites in main shopping areas, attractive window displays can be a more economic form of promotion.

5. Distributor Public Relations

How many marketing managers bother about distributor relations, beyond perhaps advertising in the trade press and that is really advertising, not public relations?

Not all products are FMCGs ordered from warehouses by supermarket managers, and even FMCGs are not sold entirely by bulk buyers. In many businesses, sales can be maintained only if retailers continue to stock them, while other products depend on the salesperson being able to explain or demonstrate them convincingly.

Dealer education is a form of public relations which marketing management neglects at its peril, yet it is surprising how often the dealer support is limited to co-operative advertising, trade deals and sales promotion. It is astonishing, for instance, how little the local salesman of a British motor-car knows about a new model compared with the salesman for a new Japanese model. It seems as if the salesman for a British motor-car is interested only in what money he will make out of selling the car, whereas the salesman for a Japanese model concentrates on value for money which the customer will enjoy. Does the BL salesman, for instance, think that the model has been pre-sold by the massive launch advertising, or even by the PR media coverage?

The dealer who knows his product exudes confidence, but how does he himself gain such confidence? He must have confidence in both the manufacturer and the product. Creating this knowledge, understanding and confidence is a positive PR objective which can have tangible results.

There are many PR techniques which can be applied such as dealer magazines, works visits, video, invitations to exhibition stands, news in the trade press and training courses. In some industries, visits - as in the travel and wine trades - can be very effective. The Japanese will take their distributors to the factory in Japan. The salesman who says 'I have seen it made,' whether it be a suite of furniture or a lawnmower, adds conviction to the advice he gives his customers.

6. Export PR

Selling abroad, the setting up of agencies or manufacturing under licence arrangements, and familiarising the overseas market or markets, requires more than salesmanship. The company, let alone the product, may be totally unknown outside the home country. It is not always recognised by management that what is a household name in Britain could by a mystery beyond the English Channel let alone beyond the oceans of the world.

The objective here, is to educate the overseas market or rather markets. For many products each country or perhaps region such as the Gulf is a separate market. Uniform world markets rarely exist.

Here is an interesting insight on this point which appeared in the Nigerian press[2]:

> '... this country is a dumping ground for several unsuitable and inferior vehicles. And the vehicles that are alright, quality-wise, often come loaded with unwanted accessories. Conversely, they do not have those items of equipment which are necessary in the Tropics.
>
> 'Cars have been imported into Nigeria for many decades and they have always come with heaters and heated rear windows. The practice continues. A heater and a heated rear window are, naturally, of no use here. The resources used to produce and fit such items of dubious value should have been employed to install more useful equipment.'

On the other hand, farm equipment is made to suit different countries and combine harvesters are designed for different crops and different working conditions and requirements.

It is rare that a product is universally acceptable, as Coca-Cola is even including its name. Many products need modifying or packaging differently to suit individual foreign markers. So with public relations. Campaigns usually have to be tailored to suit particular national or regional markets, and they must take into consideration the type of society and its needs and the kind of media that exist to reach the potential market. Press stories and pictures need a local interest angle. For instance, a newspaper in a foreign country is more likely to print a picture of a product being used in that country than a general picture taken in the producer's home country.

Much can be done in the UK through Government and other services such as the Central Office of Information, External Services of the BBC and the British Overseas Trade Borad, while EIBIS International Ltd. produce and distribute translated news stories and articles to the foreign press.

For international trade purposes the objective proposed earlier in this section may be too broad, and some more specific objectives could be:

(a) To establish the corporate image in the minds of influential people in prospective overseas markets. These could be government officials, government buying agencies, large commercial buyers, import agents, wholesalers and large distributors.

(b) To familiarise the consumer or user market with our product.

(c) To attract enquiries from prospective agents.

(d) To prepare the way for a sales visit, or to co-incide with a sales visit or trade mission or participation in a trade exhibition, again with the assistance of the BOTB and British government officials in the country or countries concerned. This could include interviews with the media, and the setting up of film or video shows and seminars.

7. Political PR

Direct political PR, from seeking the interest and support of your local MP to lobbying MPs interested in your industry (and most MPs have special interests), and Parliamentary liaison to know what is going on in Parliament such as the progress of bills or the opportunity to present evidence to a Royal Commission, may be valuable to management. But this does not include bribing Members of Parliament or senior servants, or expecting a lobby correspondent to divulge the contents of a White Paper received confidentially a day before publication. Trade associations and other representative bodies form pressure groups which lobby MPs, and government itself welcomes the opportunity to discuss its ideas and proposed legislation with such collective bodies.

This is an area of public relations which is easily misunderstood. It has nothing to do with corruption, and is a throughly reputable and recognised link in the process of government. It is quite proper to pay an MP a fee to advise a company on Parliamentary procedures, and this does not require him to take any action in favour of the company. Members of Parliament are well aware of the rules of the House in these matter. A number of Members of both houses are employed by PR consultants, and their names are disclosed in Parliamentary Registers maintained by the Institute of Public Relations and the Public Relations Consultants Association.

Some objectives may therefore be:

(a) To inform MPs about a company's case when a bill is coming before the House which affects their industry. This could be done by writing to each individual MP prior to a committee stage of the bill.

(b) To keep a Minister (and also a Shadow Minister on the Opposition bench) informed about company developments.

(c) To be kept informed of Parliamentary matters which may concern a company, e.g Questions asked in the House and answers given; impending legislation; or Royal Commissions or the Monopolies Commission. For this purpose, a PR consultancy specialising in Parliamentary liaison may be appointed.

(d) To keep the local MP fully aware of the company's activities and problems which might, for instance, involve quotas of imports by foreign rivals.

8. Consumer Relations

Sometimes management, and marketing management in particular, think this is all PR is about, but, as has been demonstrated already in this chapter, PR enters into every aspect of a business. Nevertheless, this is an area in which numberless objectives may be set, all of them being more deliberate and result-seeking than merely creating a favourable image or a favourable climate of opinion. However, they do aim to create a favourable marketing situation which is in itself tangible. Recalling some of the marketing mistakes described in Chapter Two, the primary mistake was the failure to create a favourable marketing situation. This is not unlike the artillery barrage preceding an attack.

Not all products can benefit from a build-up of educational PR. Secrecy may be vital to a successful launch, and PR may not be possible until the wraps are off. Moreover, PR does not stop with the launch. It goes on throughout the life of the product or service. Some products have a life cycle which suffers eventual decline, others receive injections and go on living, some are replaced by new models, and a few have a staircase life-cycle or new uses which perpetuate the product's life. The needs and opportunities of consumer relations will depend on the nature of the product.

To conclude this chapter here is a short list of consumer relations objectives for a product or service.

(a) To announce a new product (known as product publicity), and there may be a press reception at which the product is demonstrated.

(b) To educate the consumer market prior to a product launch.

(c) To maintain consumer or user interest in a product, such as by publishing case-history articles describing use of the product or service, or by the publication of books such as McDougalls cookery book which is now in its 29th edition.

(d) To encourage customers to make repeat purchases, or in the case of occasional purchases to buy the same make (e.g. a motor-car) next time. This is a little like maintaining interest but relies more on customers being made constantly aware of the product because it is frequently in the news for a variety of reasons.

(e) To establish the reputation of the company so that there will be a halo effect when new products are introduced and they enjoy the good name of the manufacterer or supplier. This is important with FMCGs.

(f) To attract enquires for a newly introduced product or service.

(g) To announce some changes in packaging, pricing, modification of the product or extension of the range of models, colours, sizes or flavours according to the type of product.

(h) To create a good response when, as sometimes happens, it is necessary to recall a product in which a defect has been discovered. Product recall will be discussed more fully in Chapter Eight.

In this chapter some 40 possible PR objectives have been presented. For any particular organisation, other objectives may be determined. These are result-orientated and not simply image-orientated or even favourable image-orientated objectives. The results are measurable either quantatively or qualitatively, that is to say by means of scientific research such as opinion polls or by observation when the results can be seen or experienced.

If objectives are set they are either achieved or not, or achieved to some extent. These results can be evaluated against cost. Usually, public relations will be found to be not only cost effective but economical. In certain cases, and this is often true with industrial or technical products, public relations will prove to be more cost effective than advertising.

The methods of evaluating results are outlined at the end of Chapter Five, this being the sixth element in the Six Point PR Planning Model.

REFERENCES

1. Dunk, William P and Kraut, G.A. Investor Relations: What It Isn't, *Public Relations*, IPR, London, Summer 1983.
2. Adeyanju, Banji, Building a Nigerian Car, *Sunday Concord*, Ikeja, Nigeria, August 28, 1983.

4.

THE COSTS OF PR

One of the first questions management will ask about public relations is 'What will it cost?' Management's idea of PR costs is often a large bill for lunches, dinners, drinks and hospitality in general. Fortunately, the idea of the gin and tonic PRO died a long time ago so far as the PR world is concerned, but the notion lingers on in the minds of some managers.

There is a difference between being courteous and offering someone the drink of the day, place or situation and literally attempting to corrupt them with lavish hospitality. For example, a good PRO does not seek favours of an editor by buying him a big lunch. Instead, he does the editor a favour by providing him with a good, authenticated story at the right time which he is happy to print. On the other hand, if a press party arrives at a farm on a cold morning for a press demonstration, it is thoughtful to first of all give the guests something hot to eat and drink. But the so-called junkets and jollies when journalists are over-indulged is a self-defeating exercise since the very guests will usually criticise the generosity.

The Primary PR Cost

Public relations is labour intensive. The primary PR cost is that of time, of manhours. The chief thing to budget is therefore the cost of manhours, and conversely what can be done with the available manhours according to its expertise. Obviously, the more skilled the PR practitioner - that is, how well trained, qualified and experienced he or she is - the more can be done more efficiently in the time.

A planned public relations programme, as discussed in the next chapter, has to be based on what can be done in the available time as permitted by the manhours represented by the salaries of PR staff or the fee of the PR consultant.

It is important for management to understand this. Only one thing can be done at a time, and nothing can be done properly unless it is allocated sufficient time. If the PR practitioner is expected to do this job and that job according to management's whim it is difficult to carry out a consistent, planned, objective programme aimed at achieving specific objectives. Yet it is not uncommon for management to regard the PRO as some sort of lackey who can be expected to do all kinds of odd jobs at any time. The result of this sort of abuse of the PRO's time is that in the end it is impossible to record what has been achieved, and the PRO has been engaged in so many conflicting activities that few things have been completed satisfactorily. This is not to say that the PRO should not be an adviser to the CEO, but allowance can be made for this in the work load.

It is therefore the PRO's or the PR consultant's responsibility to devise a plan over time which uses manhours efficiently. If additional work is required then extra manhours have to be provided. They can be supplied in only one of two ways: by modifying the existing programme, or by authorising extra expenditure on more staff or more consultancy service. But the same staff, or the same consultancy fee, cannot do more in the same manhours. This must be understood by both sides.

Estimating Manhours

This emphasises the need to estimate the correct volume of time, and budget the necessary funds, at the point of planning the campaign for a period such as the financial year.

It also means that a consultancy fee should not be regarded as a retainer. All a retainer does is ensure that a consultant is available to a client, after which services must be paid for. Generally, retainers are not paid in public relations, and fees relate to precise programmes.

The manhours of a staff PRO are simply his total number of working hours in a year. Admittedly, in the nature of his job, the PRO may well do a lot of unpaid overtime since salaries are not usually restricted to 'office hours', but an approximation of his available time does allow the planning of time and the volume of time (or number of staff) required.

For the PR consultant, manhours are more critical. The consultant has nothing else to sell except his time and that of his staff, valued according to its expertise and cost. Most fees are based on an hourly rate. This hourly rate covers salaries, overheads and profit. The rate may vary according to the seniority of the executive who services the client. It is therefore critical to the consultant's profitability and survival that the hourly rate is computed correctly to cover the time given to the client, and overall the manhours of the consultant and his staff will be divided economically between a number of clients. Even so, one hundred per cent of the consultancy's manhours cannot be sold because the business has to be administered and that includes investments of time in seeking new business. The hourly rate may sometimes look high, but a consultancy is fortunate if 50 per cent of its time can be charged to clients. This becomes even more critical with a very small consultancy in which, inevitably, a disproportionate amount of time has to be spent on administrating the business.

In buying consultancy services management must understand what it is paying for. Too low a fee may mean an inexperienced consultant. As in most things, one tends to get what one pays for. This also applies to the size of the fee. Compared with advertising, the cost of PR services is relatively small, but as with advertising it is necessary to spend enough money to achieve the desired result. One of the failings in the use of consultancy services can be that too little is spent to provide sufficient manhours to gain proper reward. If one buys only so many bricks one can build a wall of only a certain size.

As described in the previous chapter, an initial cost should be a communication audit to research the situation before planning a campaign. The cost of this might be around £10,000. Such an audit is an investment because without a careful appraisal of the situation, and the establishment of the current image and knowledge of what is known or thought about the company, any plans or budgets could be inappropriate and wasteful. Here we are concerned with a broad-based PR campaign and not just a press relations service.

Other Costs

In addition to the main cost of time there are two other costs.

The first consists of all materials used such as stationery, postage, photography, print, press cutting services, radio and TV monitoring, films, video and so forth.

The second is made up of expenses such as travelling, hotel accommodation, hospitality and catering.

Material costs will be high only when there are large items such as the printing of a house journal, the making of a film or, as occurs nowadays in some large companies, the operating of a video studio. But usually the latter is mainly concerned with the production of training videos, and only part of the cost is for a video house magazine.

Budgeting PR Programmes

The only difference between an in-house budget and a consultancy budget is that the consultancy's hourly rate has to contain a profit. Both can be calculated to cover all costs such as heat, light, rent, rates, insurance, depreciation on furnishings and equipment, and services. Thus it is possible to draw up annual budgets either way.

A variation is that some large consultancies charge out the salaries plus a mark up for each member of the staff employed on a campaign.

Differences Between PR And Advertising Costs

Management may be puzzled by the differences between the costs of using an advertising agency and a PR consultancy, or between advertising and PR costs generally. This requires explanation.

In advertising, the biggest cost is usually that of buying press space and airtime, followed by production costs. The first do not arise in PR, and the second are likely to be considerably less.

Although there are variations today, and the advertising agency world has changed with the advent of *a la carte* non-media-buying agencies which mostly charge fees, and media independents which may or may not charge fees, management has for a long time been used to the commission system. Under the commission system the client receives many services free of charge, such as those of the account executive. The PR consultancy has no sources of commission and has to charge for all time consumed on the client's behalf, including talking to the client as when regular, say monthly, progress meetings are held. Also, when the client wishes to consult the consultancy the time has to be paid for.

Because of the costs involved in running a consultancy, including salaries, the consultancy cannot operate on credit, and fees will be charged monthly or maybe quarterly in advance.

The Budget

When submitting a planned PR programme for a period such as a year, the PRO or PR consultant should also submit a detailed budget covering the costs for manhours (either in-house salaries or consultancy fees), together with estimates for material costs and expenses. Management should insist on proper budgets, and not be satisfied with round figure total estimates. The figures can then be matched against the proposals. Adjustments can be made until finally the budget is approved and accepted. This will form the basis of the contract of service.

Not only does the budget set out the agreed expenditure for either a single *ad hoc* job, or a complete programme over a period of time, but it limits the workload. If, in the course of the year, additional work is required by management this can be undertaken in terms of time and money only if original agreed plans are modified or there is a supplementary budget for the extra work.

On page 30 is a hypothetical consultancy budget, based on hourly rate of £40 an hour which is used simply for arithmetic reasons. The calculations show the number of hours per job, multiplied by the number of times the job is performed, multiplied by the hourly rate.

Progress meetings are those held with the client to report work in progress and expenditure to date, discuss work being undertaken, and accept any modifications that may be necessary as a result of experience or new or different requirements. Therefore, although a plan and a budget may be agreed a few months before the campaign starts, everything is flexible in the light of actual experience.

This budget is entirely imaginary but it serves to demonstrate how a consultancy fee can be calculated. To this amount must be added estimates of the various costs of materials and expenses involved, and a contingency fund of, say, 10 percent. The total might reach £30,000, to which should be added about £10,000 for a communication audit. Thus a complete figure of £40,000 is reached. But this figure could be a lot less or a lot more according to the simplicity or complexity of the campaign, and also according to the cost of appreciating the situation which may or may not require independent scientific research.

CONSULTANCY BUDGET OF MANHOURS/FEES

JOB	No. of hours	No. of times	Hourly rate	Total cost
			£	£
Monthly progress meetings	3	12	40	1440
News releases	3	12	40	1440
Feature articles	21	3	40	2520
Works visit	21	1	40	840
Press receptions	21	3	30	2520
Exhibition support	21	1	40	840
Writing, designing annual report	14	1	40	560
Writing speeches for Chairman	3	3	40	360
Maintaining press information service	250		40	10000
General management advice	100		40	4000
Arranging radio, TV interviews	4	3	40	480
				£25.000

Figure 1

Budgetary Control

The budget is not controlled simply by discussing current against budgeted expenditure at monthly progress meetings. It is a daily discipline carried out by the account executive, and this is in the interests of both the consultancy and the client. It enables the consultancy to control the expenditure of time so that both sides get value for money, no more and no less.

The account executive keeps a simple time sheet for each client with columns for each day of the week in which time is recorded for each act performed whether it be a telephone call, dictating a letter, writing a release, calling on a printer, talking to a journalist or attending a client meeting. These entries must be made as they occur, or at least within 24 hours, otherwise they will be forgotten. If the account executive is travelling about he should keep a temporary record in a diary or notebook which is later transferred to the time sheets. At the end of the week time sheets should be given to the account executive's secretary who transfers weekly totals to a monthly time sheet.

There can be certain variations according to the nature of the account. Some clients will be serviced regularly so that the monthly total should represent a twelfth of the annual workload. But other clients may have seasonal requirements, and it will then be appropriate to maintain, say, a three months time bank to allow for irregular take up of the budgeted time.

Again, it could happen that a client who makes regular use of the consultancy's time could threaten to exceed the allotted monthly total. The account executive could watch the rapidly diminishing allocation of time, and contact the client to ask whether he wishes to overrun the budgeted sum (and pay a supplementary fee) or confine himself to the agreed volume of monthly time.

Allied to this are Job Numbers, and these apply to the control of budgeted material costs and expenses. If each job, such as photography or print, is given a coded job number when an order is issued this will identify the individual job. This is important because there can be scores of jobs performed by the same suppliers whose invoices must now identify for which clients the various jobs were commissioned. These job numbers enable the consultancy to not only keep within budget, but charge out work to clients. Job numbers are also useful for the agendas of progress meetings, and also for itemising progress or contact reports (a special style of minuting which allocates personal responsibilities on both sides) as produced by the consultancy after a client meeting.

The combination of job sheets, job numbers and regular progress meetings means that there can be strict budgeting control and accurate charging out so that the client has nothing to dispute and the consultancy is fairly paid and rewarded.

These kinds of calculation, control and account rendering are ones which management can well understand, and is entitled to insist on receiving. They show that the PR practitioner is both businesslike and accountable. Management knows what it can both expect and is getting for its money.

5.

PLANNING A PR PROGRAMME

The budget discussed in the previous chapter is allied to the plan of operation, and this can be arrived at by applying the Six Point PR Planning Model on which the proposition is based. Associated with this scheme can be a graphic representation in the form of a critical path analysis or a D-Day chart. In this chapter we shall discuss the planning formula, the proposition and the charting of the programme.

Six Point PR Planning Model

This is a standard, logical procedure which has been widely adopted in PR, and it has two values:

First, it sets out the framework for a PR programme.

Second, it invites us to look at all possibilities and needs and then imposes various constraints which are not only those of the budget.

In preceding chapters some aspects of the planning model have already been dealt with in detail. Here we relate these and other aspects of planning PR programmes.

The six elements of the planning model are:

1. Appreciation of the situation, or the communication audit.
2. Defining the objectives of the PR programme.
3. Defining the publics with whom we need to communicate.
4. Defining the media through which we can reach the selected publics, and also special techniques for doing so.
5. Budgeting.
6. Evaluation of results.

1. Appreciation of the Situation

This has been discussed already in Chapter One when we considered the first part of The Mexican Statement - analysing trends - and introduced the concept of the communication audit, quoting Reginald Watts. We are concerned now with revealing the current image - what people think and know about the company. Where are we now - what is the state of hostility, prejudice, apathy or ignorance? What are our strengths and weaknesses?

Opinion or attitude tests, image studies or the communication audit are all methods of conducting investigative research. Other research can consist of observation, such as monitoring the media to learn what they are saying and how correctly, falsely, favourably or antagonistically they are doing so. Feedback from other sources such as dealers, customers and employers in the forms of praise, criticism or suggestions is also valuable. Thus, we have three chief sources of information: research, observation and feedback.

Objective Interpretation of Data

The interpretation of this intelligence must be objective and open-minded. Some of it may be surprising, not all of it will be flattering, and it will certainly be enlightening. The extent of misunderstandings and misconceptions can be a dramatic revelation, as some very big companies have discovered.

The need for a PR campaign does not really become apparent until such an assessment is made. Public relations people often criticise management for not understanding PR and for not using it properly, but the real point is that unless the communication situation has been studied how can management appreciate that anything needs to be done?

It is like going to a doctor for a medical checkup. The patient feels fine and doesn't know anything is wrong until the doctor diagnoses diabetes or some other unsuspected condition. The conditions requiring PR attention are usually unsuspected by management which has been living blissfully in a make-believe world. The current image is what people outside the company think and know about it; the mirror image is what management thinks people outside the company think and know about it. The two are very rarely identical.

The commissioning of a preliminary study is therefore a courageous step for management to take. It is more sensible than to either reject PR as unnecessary, or indulge in PR because it seems fashionable to do so, or because a management consultant has advised it - but without first finding out why it is necessary. When the problems are recognised, management is encouraged to recognise, too, that PR techniques are the means of solving these problems. Those techniques will also be recognised as being rather more than mere press relations.

Here are some typical problems revealed by enquiries to appreciate the situation:

(a) The company name suggested it was foreign, when it was really British.

(b) Because it was an American transnational, it was thought that the company was milking the national economy.

(c) Because the products were British-made, it was thought that they were inferior to long-established imported makes.

(d) Prices were thought to be too high, when they were justified by the superior quality.

(e) The company was associated with only one product, when in fact it was active in other types of business.

(f) The organisation was thought to be run by the Government, when in fact it was a charity or an independent business.

(g) The location was considered inconvenient, when it actually enjoyed many advantages.

(h) Potential employees, in a heavy industry area, thought it was beneath their dignity to work for a light industry.

(i) The company was falsely associated with some scandal or controversy, perhaps because of similarity of name or product.

From these examples it will be seen that unsuspected situations could be detrimental to business success, nullifying marketing, advertising and sales efforts. But they are typical situations which can be rectified by a planned PR programme. If the reader, thinks carefully it will be realised that all the above examples have been experienced by a number of well-known organisations.

2. Defining The Objectives

As we saw in Chapter Three, tangible public relations are based on planning a PR programme to achieve defined objectives, and in that chapter some 40 possible objectives were posed. These objectives are obtained by discussing the communication needs of different departments - personnel, production, marketing, finance as well as the corporate needs of the board. Constraints now apply because only a limited number of objectives can be entertained. Mainly, this will be because of the budget, but it is possible that commercial media may not exist to reach the particular publics and the cost of creating private media may be prohibitive. A private medium might be a documentary film or video.

The objectives will be different for each company, and they will be derived from the results of auditing the situation. In the preceding section, nine typical problems were enumerated, and each posed a possible objective, a problem to be solved.

3. Defining Publics

In advertising, sales messages are addressed to market segments and target audiences which may be large and exclusive, although the target audience for FMCGs can be the very large and extensive mass market. The opposite occurs in PR where a multitude of large and small audiences are addressed. They are known as publics and could range from school children to politicians and not necessarily be customers or users.

There is a standard list of eight publics:

(a) The community made up of those who live in the vicinity of the company's premises.

(b) Potential staff who may be located locally, in rival companies, in colleges and even overseas.

(c) Existing staff of all categories.

(d) Suppliers of services and materials.

(e) The money market, from the local bank manager to the stock market.

(f) Distributors of every kind.
(g) Consumers and users.
(h) Opinion leaders of every sort whose influence can be hostile or friendly.

For any individual business, the publics will be selections from and extensions of this basic list.

In planning a campaign it is therefore necessary to list all the groups of people - publics - with whom we wish to communicate a variety of messages for different purposes. Public relations is seldom to do with delivering messages to mass audiences, as with advertising. There could even be a public of one, if there was an individual whose understanding of the business was vital to its success. It could be an influential critic who was misinformed and dangerous in his or her ignorance.

Here is an example of the publics relevant to a large food manufacturing company. It is necessary at the planning stage to list every possible group of people with whom the company does, should or wishes to communicate. However, budgeting constraints and/or absence of suitable media are likely to demand that the list be pruned. Again, different publics may be addressed at different times in order to ration resources. Like politics, PR is the art of the possible.

PUBLICS FOR A MANUFACTURING COMPANY

The community adjacent to the factory.
Potential staff wherever they may be.
Existing staff: management, executives, office, sales, production, warehouse, transport, etc.
Trade unions, trade associations.
Suppliers of services such as local authority and professional, raw materials, ingredients, containers and packaging.
The money market: investors, brokers, investment analysts, investment institutions.
Distributors: wholesalers, retailers, bulk buyers for chains, catering establishments.
Consumers: children, housewives, special groups such as campers and caravanners.
Opinion leaders: cookery writers, dieticians, Ministry of Food and Department of Trade officials.

4. Defining Media and Techniques

How do we reach these publics? While a number of publics can be reached simultaneously through the mass media, many publics can be reached only through media addressed to them specifically or even created specially for them. Created media include house or private magazines, documentary films, video, private exhibitions and seminars, and educational print. There can therefore be both existing and created media. The diversity of PR media may be a surprise to management more used to seeing their products advertised in big circulation newspapers and magazines, networked on commercial television and displayed nationwide on the hoardings.

This is one of the reasons why journalists are not necessarily the best recruits for PR because they may have little knowledge of media outside the particular kind of journal on which they have worked. One of the greatest skills possessed by an expert PR practitioner is not how to write a publishable news release, but knowledge of the vast range of PR media and ability to use it effectively. This calls for a good working knowledge of design, printing, photography, film and video making, all of which are very different from journalism.

An analysis of media will help to explain one of the major skills which management can buy when appointing either a PRO or a PR consultant. In fact it is fair to say that one way of judging a good PR practitioner when making an appointment is to test the breadth of his or her knowledge of media. The test question is not 'Do you have good Fleet Street contacts.' Any seasoned PR practitioner will say 'No' because, if a story is worth publishing, publication can be obtained on its merits. Knowing people in the media is useful so that the PRO can have a practical working relationship, not so that favours can be demanded.

Existing Media

The Press

According to *Benn's Press Directory*[1], some 10,000 publications are published in the UK. They spread over newspapers of which 100 dailies are published outside London; hundreds of regional weeklies; consumer and special interest magazines; trade, technical and professional journals; Chamber of Trade and Commerce journals; hundreds of local freesheets; hundreds of internal and external house journals; and hundreds of specialist yearbooks and journals. The national newspapers, both daily and Sunday, are read by distinct class groups from the *Financial Times* to the *Daily Star* with the *Daily Express* and *Daily Mail* occupying a middle position in the readership social scale. Consequently, it is seldom relevant to send a story to the 'national press.'

One of the secrets of successful press relations is knowing how to write the right story for the selected media, and also knowing which few papers are likely to print it. A lot of effort and money is wasted on sending the wrong stories to the wrong media. Another skill is knowing how and when journals are printed, for there is no point in sending even a good story to a journal which, for production reasons, was printed weeks ago even though it is not yet on sale.

The British PRO has the advantage of having a vast choice of publications in which he may be able to print news, pictures or feature articles, but he has to know what they want, how they want it and when they want it. Press relations is not a matter of posting scores of news releases in broadcast fashion and hoping some will be successful. If a hundred releases are posted and one is published that is a success rate of one percent, but if only one release is sent to a paper which really welcomes it that is 100 percent success.

Management should be wary of receiving lists of publications to which news releases have been sent, together with a bill if it is a PR consultant. It is the hit rate which matters. The bill from the press cutting agency is more significant, although what is much more significant is where did the story appear, the *Pimlico Post* or the *Daily Telegraph*?

This is when management's ability to buy PR services becomes significant too. While management needs to employ skilled practitioners it is also necessary for management to be able to recognise that skill, or the lack of it. One of those management abilities is to be able to spot whether the results of a press relations exercise make sense. Is management paying for results or rubbish?

An excellent example of what management can easily recognise as a genuine report of a first class media campaign is the detailed statistical report[2] on the PR coverage of the London Marathon, which West Nally Group produce for the title and supporting sponsors. This includes press, radio and TV coverage. Mars have now taken over from Gillette as title sponsors.

Management should also be cautious of receiving collections of press cuttings, nicely mounted in albums like a stamp collection. More relevant is an assessment of where the reports appeared, together with an evaluation which can be made by giving values to different publications so that scores can be calculated for each story issued. In addition to this, by adopting either or both the circulation and readership figures (which are different) it is possible to estimate the number of people who had the opportunity to read the story. In such ways it is possible to genuinely evaluate press coverage. It is not done by calculating the cost of paying the advertisement rate for the space occupied by PR stories. That is irrelevant. Press coverage is not free advertising as we established in Chapter Two. A few column centimetres in the *Financial Times* could be more valuable than half-a-page in the *Sun*, and vice versa according to the subject.

Television

As the hours of broadcasting and the number of stations increase, so do the opportunities for PR coverage. New alternative television techniques are both changing the nature of the medium and providing more selective rather than the mass audiences of the recent past. It is unlikely that we shall ever again see a 20 million television audience like that enjoyed by the Royal Wedding on July 19, 1983.

Cable television, time shifting by taping and playing tapes back when convenient, the use of the television for playing hired or bought video-tapes, or with home computers, or for video games; and the demand information and tele-shopping facilities which will grow with the Prestel, Oracle and Ceefax systems, all promise to splinter mass audiences. This will have a drastic effect on audience figures and the ability of commercials to reach the vast audiences which existed in the 60s and 70s. Popular television may well go the way of the Odeons and other big cinemas.

This break-up of the mass television audience, and the introduction of what has become known as alternative television has been described by Alvin Toffler[3] as the demassification of the media.

Television offers an increasing number of opportunities for PR coverage, and the new trends must not be overlooked., Nevertheless, traditional BBC and ITV will still offer oportunities within the news, magazine, current affairs, documentary, serial, give-away and chat show programmes. Television is not a generality (like the national press mentioned above), and programmes have to be selected according to their relevance, remembering that some programmes are produced many months in advance so that the correct timing of an approach to a producer is essential. If one is sponsoring an event (as indicated by the report on the Gillette London Marathon) the coverage can be enormous. Likewise, sponsorships of golf, tennis, snooker, darts, horse-racing, football, cricket and motor-racing gain considerable viewing time, and one of the successes of multi-media coverage has been Cornhill Insurance's sponsorship of Test Cricket. The Canon Football League is likely to have even greater impact.

Three important points about television which will be discussed again in the next chapter are:

(a) It is predominantly an entertainment medium, even when programmes are allegedly serious.

(b) It is a visual medium watched more than listened to.

(c) Taking part in or servicing TV is immensely time-consuming. This could be a serious constraint if resources are limited.

Radio

Britain has seen a great extension of radio services since the introduction of local BBC and independent (ILR) radio stations, and their proposed number is not yet complete. The opportunities here for PR coverage are different from those of television. The medium can be more national or more local than television. It is an instant medium and far less time consuming than television in its preparation. Here the voice is important, and physical appearance is irrelevant.

CREATED MEDIA

A multitude of created media can be developed by the imaginative PR practitioner, and in the main they apply to special publics and often to small audiences. These will be discussed individually in the next chapter.

5. Budgeting

The budgeting of PR campaigns has already been explained in the preceding Chapter Four on the Costs of PR. Here, as the fifth element of the PR Planning Formula, budgeting has to be seen in relation to the other elements. It is the principal constraint on the total programme, representing as it does labour, resources, materials and expenses.

There are two ways of approaching the budget. First, what is the estimated cost of mounting a PR programme to solve communication problems. Ideally, an initial sum has been allocated to research the situation or conduct a communication audit. The programme budget can then be based on needs. However, it may be that a second way of approaching the budget is adopted, management declaring a sum of money for PR purposes. If PR is well-established in the company, the budget can be based on experience, but it would be unrealistic to impose a set budget irrespective of the need. Generally speaking, it is more realistic at all times for the budget to be proposed by the PR practitioner, even if it has to be modified. If a PR consultant is disappointed in what the client is prepared to spend, and genuinely believes that he cannot do a proper job for the money, he is entitled to withdraw his services. Because PR is mostly labour intensive, and time is the major cost factor, no programme can be conducted satisfactorily if there is insufficient manpower to cover the workload. This is one of the hardest things management has to learn about public relations.

6. Evaluating Results

The tangibility of public relations was demonstrated in detail in Chapter Three, and some 40 examples were given of possible PR objectives. Further observations on objectives are made earlier in this chapter in the comment on the second element of the planning model. If a management by objectives approach is made to public relations there must be results good, bad or indifferent. The extent of which the results are as forecast will indicate whether the plan and its execution was correct. Any failure to achieve the desired results calls for a post mortem examination. What went wrong? Were the wrong tactics or the wrong media used? Did some unforeseen influence put the programme off course? Was the budget inadequate? Assuming all went well, the results should be as forecast.

Different objectives require different methods of assessment, quantitative or qualitative. Many results can be observed or experienced, and do not call for independent scientific research. Some results can be seen in the trading figures, and some of our most successful businesses are those which make consistent use of PR. But if the objectives in Chapter Three are recalled or re-read, many of the desired results cannot be assessed in monetary terms. Many of them are outside the marketing sphere, yet they are vital to the health of a business and other activities such as marketing may not prosper if these objectives are not achieved.

Marketing Research

Let us look first at the application of marketing research techniques to the measurement of PR results. The methods used initially to assess the situation can be re-applied. An opinion survey will have a questionnaire, covering a number of things. Let us suppose that respondents were given a multiple choice question, and were asked to indicate the companies or products they knew, were familiar with, had bought or used, or had heard of. As a result of collating the answers, the following table could emerge. Let us assume our company is G. The percentages represent percentages of the sample of people interviewed. The sample can be designed to suit the subject, based on sex, age, social grade and so on.

A	10%
B	20%
C	5%
D	30%
E	15%
F	25%
G	2%
H	9%

The percentages do not total a hundred because some people will indicate more than one name. The objective of the PR campaign is to increase awareness over a period of a year, raising it from its lowly 2% to at least 15%. Following the execution of the campaign a survey can be conducted of a similarly constituted sample. There may be variations in the other figures, but it is the percentage for G which matters. If a result such as the following emerged, the campaign could be counted a success:

A	12%
B	20%
C	6%
D	30%
E	16%
F	25%
G	16%
H	10%

The figures given here are fictitious but something like that happened after Cornhill's first year of Test Match sponsorship. In addition to achieving that sort of improvement in awareness there was a corresponding sales boost and improved staff morale.

Other research techniques may be used. The image study method tests attitudes over a range of topics (e.g. service, delivery, performance, price, research), the sponsor's company being matched against a number of rival companies. A graph can then be drawn showing how each company rates on each topic, and the comparisons present an image of the company compared with that of its rivals. This could be used in the initial research, the campaign could aim to make known remedies taken in the weak areas, and a further image study could be undertaken at the close of the campaign. This method is excellent for an industrial company where the sample of typical buyers can be small but representative.

A third method is the discussion group in which a representative group is assembled and the group leader asks questions, there is a spontaneous discussion and the group leader records concensus answers. This is an inexpensive method.

Other Methods of Evaluation

By observation, it will be possible to tell whether there has been an improvement in the calibre of applicants for jobs, a share price has kept steady at a good level, or the media are showing better understanding of the company.

By experience, it will be known whether industrial friction has subsided, the sales force is being received more warmly by the trade, or there are fewer complaints.

A great many PR results of this kind will show a recognisable change from the negative states of hostility, prejudice, apathy and ignorance culminating in misunderstanding to a positive state of understanding and goodwill. This may manifest itself in many satisfactory ways such as better response to advertising, more enquiries, use of the product for other purposes or by other user groups reached by the PR, greater respect for the company by those who were previously antagonistic or sceptical, and generally better recognition of the repute of the company. These examples may be a little generalised but it would be tedious to repeat the numerous objectives listed in Chapter Three, each of which is capable of having a tangible result.

For example, we quoted in Chapter Two a number of marketing failures, some of which were converted into successes once the necessary PR was finally carried out. To expand on the Thoresen theme, a lot of projects in the holiday and travel world have benefited from the skilful use of PR. The results were obvious and needed no expenditure on research, and this is true of many PR campaigns. What could have aroused more hostility, prejudice, apathy and ignorance than the idea of a winter weekend in Moscow? Yet Thomson Holidays, by taking a press party to Moscow on a sample weekend, achieved such a volume of press coverage that they were able to literally break the ice and successfully launch cheap weekend holidays to Moscow in mid-winter!

Thomson Holidays, with a team of only three headed by Douglas Goodman, has so consistently used PR tactics over the past ten years that they have been a recognised contribution to the company's growth to number one in the trade. In November 1982 bookings had fallen to only a third of the previous year, but aided by PR the holiday brochure was re-launched with more competitive offers. By January record bookings were being taken.

Here is Douglas Goodman's account[4].

The most important events in the tour operator's year are the launch of new holiday programmes. For the marketing departments this means starting the detailed planning over a year before the first clients travel and while the existing year's programme is barely under way.

The objectives for the launch of Summer 1983 were precise: to create maximum awareness on launch day of the Summer Sun, Lakes and Mountains, Small and Friendly, Coaches, and Villas and Apartment holidays. Five different programmes were to be launched on 1 September in 5 million brochures. Over 890,000 holidays would be offered from May to October 1983 to 28 countries from 16 UK airports.

The date was set over three months in advance to allow all the activities to be properly planned: the £1 million advertising campaign; the three-day sales conference in Birmingham; the briefing and training of all staff; a travelling road show visiting 16 cities; the printing and distribution of the brochures; and the public relations work which would occupy most of August.

Preparations for the launch involved: choosing the venues for the 10 press conferences and booking the catering; preparing the invitation list; checking the mailing lists; deciding upon the key points for news and feature stories; preparing scripts and 10 different slide presentations for the press conferences; writing national and local news releases; researching facts on new destinations; arranging for releases in appropriate foreign languages; commissioning tapes; and staging rehearsals. A road show with a giant trailer and a fleet of transit vans would visit 16 cities to provide a sophisticated audio-visual presentation for 5,000 travel agents. The PR department planned to accompany this to gain local publicity a few weeks after the launch. A personality girl had to be found and photographed on location for the launch.

Fortunately August is traditionally a quiet month for travel publicity - that is, unless any disasters happen. June is usually the 'silly season' for the press and in September interest in travel begins again with the launch of new programmes and the start of winter sports publicity. The Thomson PR team prayed that August would not be exceptional!

First Out

Thomson is traditionally the first company to launch its brochure. Most holidaymakers know exactly when they want to go abroad: factory weeks are set and they have decided where they want to go. To the tour operator, therefore, early sales are vital. The more you can 'get in' before competitors launch their programmes the better and in the first week that the brochure was on sale in September 1981 over 60,000 rushed out to book with Thomson. Queues really did form outside some travel shops!

The disadvantage of being first out is that other operators can see Thomson's prices before finalising their own and then when they launch they can undercut Thomson prices in hotels which the companies share. This gives any operator a major marketing advantage to use to the full in advertising and public relations activities. In late 1982 Thomson was, for once, ready to tackle this move by its competitors in a positive and unprecedented way.

The Summer '83 brochures were launched on 1 September. Next day five national papers, BBC Radio, the provincial press and provincial radio, and the travel press all gave Thomson extensive and satisfactory publicity. The battle began in earnest later in September as other operators began to launch their '83 brochures: prices for identical holidays were cheaper in their rivals' brochure - by more than had been expected - and the contingency plan was put into action.

Surcharges, an unpleasant but accepted part of package holidays, have been with us for a number of years. As overseas costs rose through a weakening pound, tour operators were compelled to pass this on to their customers as a maximum 10 percent surcharge. In October, when a major operator launched and guaranteed 'no surcharges', Thomson matched the offer within hours and gained further publicity for its own programme.

By November the travel industry sensed that something was wrong. The early bookings were just not materialising. September, October and November - months which usually provided steady bookings - were poor. Business was down about 30 per cent over the previous year.

The weeks after Christmas had always been the peak booking season when operators expected to sell about half their holidays. The previous two years had seen a move towards later bookings and the press actively encouraged people to hold back and wait for last-minute bargains.

With Autumn sales slow, tour operators wondered if the summer package tour, up to then a top priority for disposable income, had finally been hit by the recession. Was 1983 to be the year when everyone stayed at home? Would January and February sales be low?

Market Stimulation

As market leader, Thomson was determined to take the initiative. Travel agents, whose cash flow was suffering, asked the company what could be done. Thomson had to stimulate the market to encourage people to book and to regain the price initiative.

With a print run of over three million main brochures the work has to be done in stages by the printing company in Italy. One million brochures had been ready for the launch in September and by December had all been distributed by agents. Another one-and-a-half million were needed for the December and January peak.

The Thomson contingency plan all along had been to reprint and re-launch the brochure if necessary, with lower prices. This would make the company's holidays so price competitive that no other operator would be able to follow suit. The second advantage, one that could not have been predicted in early summer, was that a re-launch would give the holiday business a tremendous boost.

In great secrecy the 320-page colour brochure was reprinted with reductions between £10 and £50 on no less than half-a-million holidays. Almost every page carried a new price panel and the cover was reprinted with the 'no surcharge' guarantee as well as the announcement of lower prices. The brochures were brought to a 'secret' warehouse in London, key staff were briefed and plans finalised.

In a business where competition is so strong, no hint of a re-launch could be allowed to leak out. The slightest word to the press that Thomson was planning something would have alerted the competition and given them time to react.

Press Reaction

Creating the awareness of the re-launch depended on the public relations and advertising activities. Maximum press coverage was needed from re-launch day, Monday 6 December until press advertising began three days later.

News stories for the national press and local versions of them were written for the provincial media, rehearsals held and all the probable questions anticipated and answered.

A suite at the Savoy was booked privately for the press conferences to be held on the Monday. Key Fleet Street writers were invited late on the previous Friday, and during the weekend, to attend a champagne breakfast at 8.30am and editors of the travel press were invited to a similar event. The combination of the Savoy and Thomson calling a conference at such short notice worked well: there was 100 per cent attendance.

It was essential to gain coverage in that day's evening papers, radio and TV news bulletins to ensure that the following day's nationals and provincials carried the news. Consequently a detailed schedule of hand deliveries, phone calls and wire stories was planned and carried out to ensure maximum impact.

It had been decided that the person to be offered for all radio and TV interviews and the name to be quoted in the press would be the company's new managing director, John MacNeill. First to carry the news was LBC which broadcast an interview with him. IRN then syndicated a story and provincial radio stations called in the local Thomson spokespeople. Radio Four's 'World at One' sent a car to collect John MacNeill and Radio 2 'Newsbeat' also wanted an interview. The lunch time ITN News carried a long report and Channel 4 news wanted help. Then things really livened up!

BBC TV arrived at head office and filmed an interview which was used on the nine o'clock news. National press wanted more comment and different National press wanted more comment and different angles to follow up. *Evening Standard* boards announced the re-launch and the paper gave prominent coverage to the news.

The day the PR department will never forget was Thursday 7 December. It was the day when Thomson achieved more press coverage than ever before. Every national ran the story - some front page - and the quality of coverage was amazing. Between them the nine nationals mentioned Thomson 72 times and several of the provincials ran the story as front page headlines. Press and radio coverage continued throughout the week. The *Financial Times* ran a perceptive piece and the *Sunday Times* devoted a whole page to the re-launch. National holiday programmes on radio and TV spread the word. Competitors' reaction was predictable. They claimed it was a 'panic move' and that Thomson had got its prices wrong first time. More publicity resulted. The awareness had been created and no other operator could reprint its brochure.

The press coverage had been so extensive that some of the national press advertising was cancelled because it was felt that awareness was so high. This was measured at the end of the lauch week in an independent survey. Recall, it was discovered, was phenomenally high and there was a stronger disposition towards buying a Thomson Holiday.

The travel press devoted much space to the event and travel agents welcomed and praised the re-launch.

One major operator did respond by reducing its prices just before Christmas. A radio interview with its spokesman began by asking if it had been panicked into the move by Thomson!

The press coverage on Thomson continued throughout December and January and the market really did pick up. An analysis of the media coverage from the original launch in September to Christmas showed that Thomson had gained four national TV and 13 national radio items, 45 national press reports, 66 regional radio interviews or news items, over 350 news items in the provincial press, extensive coverage in the travel press and many items in magazine and foreign press. The value of the coverage gained, in advertising cost, totalled £115,000 but neither the figures for cuttings nor the theoretical value reflect the quality of the coverage.

Many travel writers praised the Thomson move and began to encourage readers to book early to take advantage of the 'early' price reductions. In January the respected trade journal *Travel Agency* said:

"Thomson's timing was, of course, spot on, allowing its competitors no time to react before Christmas," and, it continued, "Whatever the reality, the Thomson ploy, manipulated to its maximum public relations advantage, caused a bit of a stir at the right time."

Record bookings were taken in January and by the end of the month business had picked up dramatically. The pace had been dictated by Thomson and Summer '83 looked set to be another good year.

Whether people would have booked in January without the re-launch will never be known but the Thomson public relations people like to think that they had something to do with it!

Finally, here is another and very different true example. Some years ago Rentokil decided to tackle the local government market, aiming to sell the authorities pest control services. The LAs were notoriously opposed to employing commercial services, preferring to do things themselves. A PR campaign was launched in two ways. Articles were published in the municipal press describing how the company had serviced some local authorities. A group of company scientists, supported by documentary films, toured the UK and ran one-day schools for public health inspectors and medical officers of health and senior members of their staffs. Within two years Rentokil services and products had been taken up by a large number of local authorities. In the 80s a major annual contract is for rodent control on the Isle of Man.

Rentokil is a company which has applied almost every known PR tactic to the development of one of Britain's most successful growth companies. Peter Bateman has directed Rentokil PR for the past 21 years. The results are very obvious. Pest control, hygiene, property preservation and other services cannot be sold unless people understand the causes of infestations and decay and how they can be eradicated or cured. Rentokil has found market education, good products and good service more meaningful than advertising which it has also used modestly. A typical end-result was the headline RENTOKIL ROCKETS in the city section of *The Guardian*[5] on August 24, 1983, reporting the company's increased interim dividend.

Charting a PR Programme

The presentation of the programme in simple, visible chart form imposes a discipline on the execution of the programme, and this can be read alongside the budget. Critical path and D-Day charts can be produced as wall charts and displayed so that everyone can see that the scheme is being progressed on time. Construction firms use critical path analysis charts in site manager's offices and elsewhere. If a vertical line is drawn from the start to the finish of the programme, the duration of tasks can be shown in shapes to the left and right of the vertical line. A very simplified version for the production of a quarterly house journal might look like Fig. 2 on page 48, but it could be elaborated to an annual chart too detailed to be reproducible on a page of this book.

The D-Day method lends itself to the detailed timetable of a single event or job, so that D-30 would represent the beginning of a month (or D-90 the beginning of three months) leading up to the day when the event happens or the job has to be completed, this being D-Day. Vital to this sort of charting is the fact that the D-Day is unalterable. Again, to stay within the confines of the page, a D-Day chart for a month is suggested here, perhaps for a press reception organised at rather short notice.

D-DAY PLANNING CHART

FOR A PRESS RECEPTION

D-30	PRO and CEO agree date and time of reception. Plan programme for press reception, e.g. reception, talk by CEO, demonstration, video presentation, buffet. Seek printer's quotation for invitation card.
D-29	Consider venues. Visit if necessary. Invite quotations.
D-28	Compile guest list. Check names.
D-25	Book venue. Design invitation card. Agree wording. Receive and agree printer's quotation and order cards and envelopes.
D-24	Photograph product being demonstrated. Order samples. Write CEO's speech and submit for approval. Order self-adhesive lapel badges, press kit wallets, visitors book. Book equipment such as VCR, microphone.
D-23	Receive CEO's approved speech. Write news release.
D-20	Receive cards and envelopes from printer. Send advance invitations to radio/television news editors.
D-19	Receive contact prints of photographs. Order prints.
D-18	Order studio artwork such as tent cards for speakers, displays, directoral signs.
D-15	Address and despatch invitations. Receive photographs.
D-10	Record acceptances, refusals. Follow up non-replies, important refusals.

D-8 Make any special or separate arrangement required by radio/television, e.g. CEO to visit radio station for studio interview.
D-3 Give venue numbers for catering, seating, together with room plan. Receive art work.
D-2 Produce copies of CEO's speech, news release, photo captions. Caption photos. Assemble press kits.
D-1 Deliver materials, equipment to venue. Prepare room. Rehearsal with CEO and demonstrator. Run through video.
D-DAY Press reception.

These together with the budget, simple budgetary control methods such as time sheets and job numbers, and concise reporting methods such as contact reports, comprise typical aspects of the practical and businesslike procedures necessary to efficient administration of an objective, planned, result-orientated public relations programme.

The Proposition

When appointing a PR consultant, and inviting proposals, the client is entitled to receive a written proposition setting out a detailed scheme and costings on the lines of the Six Point PR Planning Model. To this would be added additional information such as a statement about the consultancy's background and experience, a note on the personal experience and qualifications of the account executive who would handle the account, an explanation of the method of payment, and perhaps a 'brag sheet' listing clients who have been or are serviced by the consultancy. If relevant, samples of work may be included. The whole should be bound in a neat but not lavish binder. Sufficient copies should be supplied for client executives who may also be involved in the appointment, such as the PR Manager, Marketing Manager, Company Secretary, Export Manager and so on.

Similarly, the in-house PRO should present his proposals for the forthcoming year in the form of a written proposal setting out his recommendations and costings.

REFERENCES

1. *Benn's Press Directory*, UK and overseas volumes, Benn Publications Ltd., Tunbridge Wells, Kent, annually.
2. *The 1983 Gillette London Marathon*, Report and Survey for Sponsors, West Nally Group, London, May, 1983.
3. Toffler, Alvin, *The Third Wave*, Pan books, London, 1981.
4. Goodman, Douglas, Thomson Holidays, *Public Relations*, Longman Group, Harlow, Summer 1983.
5. *The Guardian*, Rentokil Rockets, Financial Guardian section, London, August 24, 1983

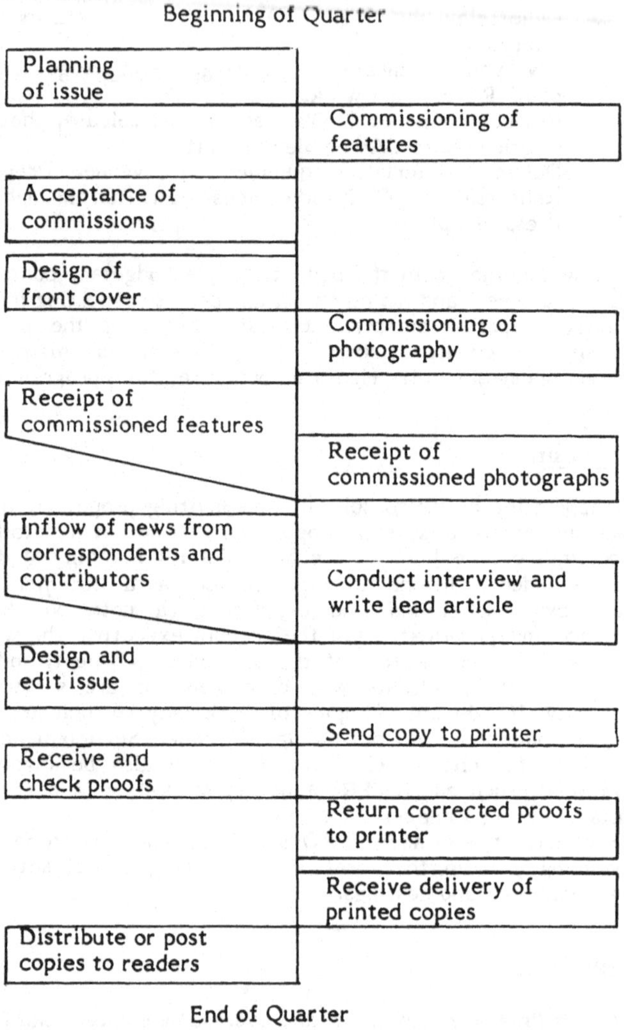

Beginning of Quarter

End of Quarter

(The vertical line will be divided into the dates when each job should begin and be completed, and each box will represent the days allocated to each job)

Figure 2 CRITICAL PATH ANALYSIS

6.

MEDIA AND METHODS

In the previous chapter a brief introduction was necessary in describing the Six Point PR Planning Model. Now let us analyse the characteristics of the various forms of existing and created media, and the methods of dealing with them or applying them during the execution of the PR programme.

As stated in the previous chapter, understanding the media is an essential PR skill and consequently management will enjoy a better understanding of PR if it also has an appreciation of communication media. This will help management to understand the tactics proposed in a prospective PR programme, and also how to co-operate with the media when personally involved as a spokesman.

The PRO or PR consultant may be the company spokesman at times, but the CEO should not hide behind them. Journalists often accuse PR practitioners of being barriers between them and management, and sometimes management - perhaps out of some unnecessary dread of the media - tend to shelter behind their PR managers or consultants. This is unwise, and competent management should be confident about dealing with the media. They can do so only if they understand how the media work.

Some management even keeps PR at arms length as if PR has nothing to do with them, and lesser mortals are hired to conduct such distasteful or menial duties. The CEO with a taste for PR is one of the greatest assets any company can have, as is shown by the successful records of companies where this is the case.

Actual media relations techniques will be discussed in the next chapter.

The Press

With such a vast and varied press in the UK, and also in most other large industrial countries, this influential medium provides the means of reaching not only very large readerships but also readers interested in almost any imaginable topic. Publics can be addressed quickly through morning and evening newspapers, and evening newspapers are published in most large regional cities. A story published in national newspapers can be on the nation's breakfast table. The power of the press is impressive in its coverage of a literate nation.

This power can be valuable or dangerous according to whether press coverage produces good or bad publicity. The latter results from two conditions: genuine bad news or misreporting because editors and their staffs do not possess the correct facts. Let us consider these two conditions from the PR point of view because they often concern management very seriously. They encourage management to mistrust the press, believing it to be deliberately perverse and mischievous.

Bad News

If something has gone wrong, a company has behaved badly, there has been a product failure or a disaster, or financial losses have been suffered, bad news coverage cannot be avoided. A good PR philosophy is to accept that there are good days and bad days. That is life. No-one can expect the news to be continually favourable, or that only favourable news will be printed. Does management accept this bitter truth? Or does it prefer to wear blinkers, even be blind-folded?

Management has no control over the press or any other mass media. It has no rights, beyond legal ones such as protection from libel, and can expect nothing except that if it does anything of interest to a large number of people its activities are likely to be reported. In today's political-economic situation, what interests a large number of people may well be redundancies, factory closures or relocations, financial losses and deals with foreigners like the Japanese. None of this is likely to be good news.

Moreover, the press is a business, not a public service or a philanthropic institution. Different publishers will print whatever will sell their papers. Management may not like this when it affects them unfavourably, but they themselves can sell only what the market will buy. We have only to look at the circulations of national newspapers to see that different numbers of people buy certain journals. A minority buy *The Times* and a majority buy the *Sun*, something like 350,000 compared with 4 million. Management may prefer *The Times* and dislike the *Sun* which may in turn be read by most of their employees, or perhaps their customers. Media, and their contents, have to be understood in the same terms as the purchase of, say, Rolls-Royce motor-cars and Austin Metros.

However, the worst effects of bad news can sometimes be modified by means of PR, and management can play a big part in this. The best way to minimise bad news is to make a frank and honest statement as quickly as possible.

Occasionally there may be legal or insurance constraints on admitting liability, but generally more good than harm will come from stating the facts, at least as presently known. So, within sensible limits, the press should be told what has happened, but not in the guarded, cynical fashion of the Tass report on the shooting down of a Korean airliner by a Russian fighter jet in August 1983. If one does not make an early statement, the story will drag on while journalists speculate and hunt the withheld information.

Management should never at any time say 'No Comment'. It is always possible to give some courteous reply, if only to explain why for the moment information is subjudice and may prejudice what is going on or other people's interests. The late general secretary of the TUC, Victor Feather, was an expert at making impressive press statements which actually said very little, but he gave them something they could print.

Misreporting

The second condition, misreporting, could be provoked by bad PR. Newspapers are produced at great speed, and editors and their staffs have to deal with facts as they have them. Sources are expected to be reliable and there may be little time in which to check them. The readers, unfortunately, think the press in infallible. There was a period when *The Guardian* printed an apology almost every day. One of the most reliable sources of press information is the PRO because it is in his own interests to supply accurate information, and he has the time and facilities to check his facts.

Sources of Press Information

Newspapers receive information from the following sources, many of which can be routes for PR stories.

(a) Staff reporters who are assigned by the news editor to cover stories.

(b) Feature writers, columnists and special correspondents who specialise in topics such as industrial relations, science, shipping, politics, including Lobby Correspondents who have special access to Parliamentary matters such as White Papers.

(c) News agencies which supply 'wire services', e.g. Reuters covering foreign news and the Press Association covering UK news. These are owned collectively by newspapers. There is also Universal News Services which operate the other way round, supplying business news from its subscribers to the press. The latter is used by PR practitioners to distribute news to the national, regional and overseas press.

(d) The syndication services of the publishers, including foreign ones, which sell material for re-publication, e.g. a *Washington Post* article which appears in *The Guardian*.

(e) Specialist private news agencies which supply features, e.g. articles, picture stories, crossword puzzles and cartoons.

(f) Authors agents and book publishers who offer the work of their clients or authors, e.g. short stories and articles, or books for serialisation.

(g) Photo agencies which cover events, and supply photographs to newspapers which pay reproduction fees for the pictures they print.

(h) News releases, pictures and feature articles from PR sources.

(i) Press conferences, receptions and facility visits organised by

PR practitioners. Also, press facilities at exhibitions and conferences.

From this extensive list it will be seen that the inflow of information to editors can be enormous, but since space is limited there has to be very careful selection of what shall be published.

To a large extent, the contents of newspapers and magazines are planned and commissioned some time in advance, or at least the publication is subdivided into sections such as home news, foreign news, women's page, leader page, arts page, city page (or section) sports page (or section), and there will be special columns, diaries and items such as Bingo contests or crossword puzzles. Mapped out like this, even a 40-page issue is reduced to half a column for this topic or a quarter page for that. The regular reader becomes familiar with the positioning of every item.

All this implies that the amount of space available for any PR story is limited by the inflow of competing material (including other news releases), and also by the space which is allocated for the sender's topic.

Very few PR stories are of the 'hard news' kind which make the front page or home news pages. Mostly, they will interest the women's page, new products page, motoring column, or City page as the case may be. It is important that the PR story shall be of interest and value to readers of the publications to which it is sent, and even then a perfectly acceptable story may get squeezed out simply because of lack of space.

It may be very difficult for management to accept these facts of life, yet criticism of the PRO's failure to publish a story may be unfair. And as we shall see in the next chapter, management could have interfered so much in the writing of an 'approved' story that they killed it before it was ever sent out. Management may simply have approved the unpublishable.

Specialised News

Management should also be aware of another limitation which is that only some newspapers carry certain kinds of news. It is therefore silly to send newspapers material which they never publish. Editors regard PROs as being ignorant when such irrelevant material is received. For instance, only a minority of newspapers will report the appointment of a CEO, and as they themselves can see by looking at the appointments feature in *The Times* and the *Financial Times*, each appointment is given only two or three lines. Yet management must have connived at the production of those three or four page life stories, and posed for portraits, which editors receive every day and direct to their rightful places, the waste paper bin. All that is required is a one-sentence statement. This is welcomed by editors who print appointment stories, and it can usually be printed as it stands. Longer stories can be written for those journals which are willing to print them, such as the CEO's professional journal or his local newspaper.

Television

This is a medium which has to be treated with care, remembering that in Britain there are two kinds, non-commercial BBC and commercial ITV. Contrary to a commonly held misunderstanding, the BBC may be more willing to make commercial references than ITV. This is because ITV producers have to be careful not to offend their advertisement departments by appearing to give 'free publicity' to commercial subjects. We have also outlived the time when in, say, TV drama, a label on a product was deliberately obscured, and it has become accepted that it is more realistic when a character in a play pours sauce from an HP bottle or whisky from a Johnnie Walker bottle, Recognisable branded products have become legitimate props.

However, care needs to be taken for the following four reasons:

1. Television can be time-consuming since it may take hours or even days to produce an item which may result in very short periods of screen time. Is management prepared to sacrifice this time, or allow members of the staff (including the PRO) to do so? The likely PR value of the programme is the criterion here.

2. There is rarely any opportunity to preview what is going to be televised, and the final result could be disappointing, perhaps exasperating. When a programme is edited, the company spokesman may find that instead of appearing in a continuous sequence as during the filmed interview, the programme is broken up and he appears in segments in juxtaposition with someone else who expresses contradictory views. He may have known nothing about the interview with his opponent.

3. The CEO may accept an invitation to be interviewed on television, and although he goes along to the studio prepared to make certain statements in his company's interests he may find that the interviewer gives him no opportunity to say what he wants to say. Instead, he is obliged to answer questions which are asked mainly to entertain the audience. They may be personal or controversial questions which are difficult to answer.

4. Television can crucify an insincere person, or one who lacks confidence when asked awkward questions. And as we have said in Chapter Five, television is predominantly a visual medium. It is therefore essential that the CEO (or any company spokesman) should look interesting on the small screen. By 'interesting' we do not necessarily mean handsome or beautiful.

These warnings are uttered because management may be tempted to want to appear 'on the box' without realising what it implies. Many a wise PRO has advised management to resist this temptation. However, we will come to this again when discussing media relations techniques in the next chapter.

PR Opportunities on Television

Now let us consider some of the opportunities for using TV as a PR communication media.

(a) *News programmes.* There are three kinds of TV news programmes, ITN or BBC national news, the local news put out by each recognised station, and special news programmes such as BBC-2's *Newsnight.* A story obviously has to be of national interest to be networked by ITN, and of major interest to feature in a special news programme. Regional news programmes often carry PR stories about companies in their area, such as a report on an unusual export order.

(b) *Magazine programmes.* These are regular programmes on certain subjects, which may be appropriate to the region such as farming, or of national interest such as those on money, new inventions, cookery, motoring, photography or gardening. Magazine programmes can be excellent outlets for PR Material, especially regarding new products and services, or answers to problems encountered by viewers.

(c) *Discussion programmes and chat shows.* A number of CEOs with interesting personalities have appeared on such shows, and they get re-invited when their programmes are enjoyed by viewers. They are usually people who are able to present serious points of view in an entertaining way. Some very big names, leaders of industry, have become television personalities.

(d) *Give-away shows.* When prizes are awarded they are seldom named, but if they are physically recognisable it is a good idea to suggest them to producers. They cannot be given to programmes, but are bought if the idea is accepted.

(e) *Properties.* When dressing sets for television drama many items are required, and some such as clocks and vacuum cleaners or items on a breakfast table can be visibly identified. All these properties are stored in studio property rooms to which a company could supply its products if they are likely to be used. Other properties can be those used in television films and series, for example the motor-cars supplied by Ford and acknowledged in the credits.

(f) *Film and videotape.* Television programmes may welcome existing material which can be used in part or whole, especially in documentaries. Archival film may be useful, as supplied for instance by Visnews. Some companies, such as airlines, shoot 'library shots', which can be inserted in television films when there are flight sequences.

From the above it will be seen that television offers unique opportunities for PR coverage, very different from those of any other medium. Credits may be given for the supply of products or services. But sometimes television producers may make unreasonable requests to film sequences on company premises - say, in a factory, bank or store - and the audience will be unware of whose premises they are, although a lot of company time has been consumed in providing the facility. On the other hand, in a *Gemima* series the heroine took tea in the palm court of the Waldorf Hotel in London which was both recognisable and later referred to by name.

Radio

Quite different again, radio, with its numerous national and local stations offers a mixture of opportunities for PR coverage which is taken up very seriously by some organisations, some of which have direct links with radio stations. The advantages of radio are that it is an instant medium through which news can be transmitted quickly. Radio is not time consuming like television, and it is very simple to make broadcasts either live in the studio, by means of pre-taped interviews or over the telephone.

PR Opportunities on Radio

Some of the PR opportunities are these:

(a) *News.* Especially in London with LBC, there are frequent news bulletins.

(b) *Studio interviews.* If one has a good topic this can be suggested to a producer, and an interview can be conducted by appointment in the station studio.

(c) *Taped interviews.* This method is used for many PR stories, provided the interview is of interest to a large audience.

(d) *Phone-ins.* These are also possible with a number of radio programmes which invite telephone participation. Company spokesmen can express points of view on topics under discussion. Again, a telephone interview or contribution may be pre-arranged with a speaker who cannot visit the studio for a live broadcast.

(e) *Topics for serials.* Topical subjects can sometimes be suggested to the writers of scripts of radio serials.

An example of a PR use of radio is on the occasion of a press reception. A radio reporter is unlikely to sit through a press reception, but he might be willing to meet the CEO in his office and tape record an interview, or the CEO could visit the studio and be interviewed about the subject of the interview. This is especially possible in London with the existence of the LBC news and discussion programmes.

Exhibitions

Public relations enters into exhibitions in two ways, and there are two kinds of exhibition, public or trade exhibitions and private ones.

Public and Trade Exhibitions

First, with public and trade exhibitions held at exhibition centres such as Olympia, Earl's Court and the National Exhibition Centre, there are many opportunities for PR coverage. They help to enhance the value of the exhibit, carrying the exhibitor's message far beyond the event itself to people who may either be encouraged to attend or who, for various reasons, are unable to attend. Big exhibitions such as motor shows are popular topics with the mass media.

To gain coverage, or representation in press features and broadcast reports, it is necessary to plan well ahead. If the official opener is to visit the company's stand, this will not be a whim or an accident. But none of this is possible by making last minute efforts. A great many exhibitors ignore the PR opportunities, yet spend large sums of money on renting stand space, designing stands, transporting exhibits, manning stands and providing hospitality. The PR opportunities cost little by comparison, except of course time, but can be very rewarding.

It is necessary to plan exhibition PR from the moment the stand space is booked. Management should be greedy about exploiting the PR opportunities which exhibitions offer, and this applies not only to the CEO but also to marketing, advertising, sales and export managers who are usually involved.

The first move is to contact the PRO of the exhibition who is usually looking for information which he can exploit to gain advance publicity for the event. Many exhibitions have an international appeal, and the exhibition PRO will be anxious to send translated stories overseas as early as possible. The exhibitor may not at this stage wish to disclose what he will be showing, but he can provide information about his business in general.

The official opener will also be known, and if the exhibit is likely to interest this VIP an approach can be made direct to this person, inviting him or her to include the stand in his or her itinerary. This early approach is necessary because during a short tour of a show the official opener has time to visit only a small number of stands.

It also pays to inform the Central Office of Information if the exhibitor is showing something new which has export possibilities. The COI may film the event, or tape interviews with exhibitors, or it may send news stories overseas. In these ways coverage can be gained in TV, radio, and press media world-wide. Similarly, the External Services of the BBC may be interested in transmitting a story about the new product, and this may go out in English and foreign language broadcasts.

The exhibitor should also take advantage of journals which are carrying reports on the exhibition, and it is not necessary to buy advertising space to support editorials. A good report will cover all the most interesting exhibits, and some will do a stand-by-stand report.

Press day and the services of the press room should not be neglected, making sure that good factual news releases and interesting photographs are supplied to the press room. The mistake should not be made of putting press material (and perhaps a lot of unnecessary sales literature) in an elaborate press kit. Visiting journalists are looking for publishable stories which they can slip in their pocket or brief case. Some exhibition press officers are sensible enough to ban press kits because of the bother they cause in disposing of them at the close of the exhibition. Journalists do not have to be impressed. They want stories. This is also a budgetary consideration since much money can be wasted on unwanted press kits.

Unfortunately, the PR opportunities of exhibitions are overlooked because the stand is supervised by marketing, sales or advertising people who have little time for PR, and here is an occasion when PR-minded management should secure the maximum PR coverage by insisting that these opportunities are not disregarded. It is an inexpensive exercise, of particular value to industrial and technical firms whose products interest the media. Such companies may not be large enough to employ a full-time PRO, but this is an occasion when it would pay to use a PR consultant on an *ad hoc* basis. Even if this is not done, it is a simple matter to telephone the exhibition PRO and ask his advice on what can be done.

Private Exhibitions

The second form of exhibition PR is the private exhibition organised for PR purposes, and this can take many forms such as:

(a) *Permanent exhibitions.* Here we have an exhibition set either on company premises, or occupying their own space or building. A well-known private show in London is the Broadcasting Gallery at the Knightsbridge offices of the Independent Broadcasting Authority. Famous ones in Europe are Philip's Evoluon science exhibition held at Eindhoven in Holland, and Lego's Legoland children's park in Billund in Denmark which attracts a million visitors a year.

(b) *Mobile exhibitions.* Almost every mode of transport has been used for mobile exhibitions including ships, trains, aircraft, buses, caravans and custom-built vehicles. They can be toured, parked at outdoor events like agricultural shows, gymkhanas, flower shows, sports events and at holiday resorts, and also taken to the continent by the many ferry services.

(c) *Portable exhibitions.* These have infinite opportunties ranging from foyers of hotels and theatres, public libraries, concourses of railway stations, press receptions, seminars, and as window displays at premises of building societies and other companies which normally have rather mundane window displays.

House Journals

There are two kinds of house journal, internal and external, and it is unwise to try to make an essentially internal staff publication serve a dual purpose. Their format can include wall newspapers, newsletters, newspapers and magazines. With the advent of web-offset printing, many house journals changed from magazine format to tabloid newspaper. Possibly because off-set printing including web-offset (using reels instead of sheets of paper), is nowadays supplied with good surface papers, the trend is swinging back to magazine format. Generally speaking, the tabloid suits the company which needs a popular style newsy newspaper for a large number of staff who prefer tabloid newspapers like the *Daily Mirror*, *Sun* and *Daily Star*, while the magazine suits the company with a more intellectual staff who enjoy reading articles.

Internal House Journals

Improved management-employee relations are resulting in journals in which there is more reader participation including the publication of critical readers letters, articles presenting workers' points of view and sales and wants advertisements.

House journals should be regarded by management as an essential form of management-employee relations. They can have added value when either posted to or taken into employee's homes. The publication should be regarded as neither a pulpit for management exhortations, nor as a paternal gift to the staff. The editorship should be independent, and not dominated by management or bogged down by editorial boards or committees. Management which insists on approving copy and proofs is getting in the way of good management-employee relations. The dead hand of official editorial boards can destroy the participatory nature of a house journal which should be an expression of industrial democracy.

In large organisations where house journals are recognised as a vital communications link, upwards and downwards, professional editors are given a free hand and management does not see the contents until they are printed. A good example is *Ford News*, edited by Derek Stone at Dagenham, which has a fortnightly circulation of 80,000 copies distributed to employees in numerous UK locations (with a special Liverpool edition), some 20,000 pensioners, and externally to journalists who are interested in Ford's internal affairs. This is by no means a recent innovation. Ford's tradition of upwards communications was pioneered more than 30 years ago when Maurice Buckmaster[1] (of SOE wartime fame) was the company's first PRO and launched *Ford News*. He introduced a feature 'Take it to the Top' in which employees could express complaints. He also insisted on communications continuing with retired staff who should receive the house journal, a policy which is still maintained.

External House Journals

External house journals are another breed altogether. They are valuable as a means of direct and regular communication with defined readership outside the organisation. The glossy prestige magazine addressed to no-one in particular is an extravagant aberration of the past.

Even so, in the USA hard-working external magazines addressed to distributors, brokers and customers have existed for more than a hundred years, to mention only those of Singer Sewing Machines and the Travelers insurance company. This is therefore one of the oldest forms of public relations.

An interesting, professionally designed and well-printed journal - that is, one of similar standard to a commercially published magazine - can be an effective way of communicating with users, customers, clients and patrons. One of the best examples is the in-flight magazine found in the pocket on the back of the aircraft seat, but there are many variations such as children's magazines published by building societies and toothpaste manufacturers, and highly technical publications issued by engineering and electronic companies.

For the exporter, the external could have an international circulation and be of great benefit to readers in developing or smaller countries where there are few magazines. Moreover, the external could be more cost-effective than taking advertising space in a lot of mediocre journals of limited circulation in overseas markets. It can have a direct mail personalised effect.

Video Magazines, Electronic Newspapers

The VCR has made it possible to show videotapes to audiences throughout a company's many locations, including those abroad or at sea in the case of oil tankers. Being small, the cassette can be posted anywhere.

A number of companies now have their own video studios and, among other things produce regularly monthly or quarterly magazines which employees can watch on TV sets in offices, canteens and other places, not usually as assembled audiences but as the opportunity occurs. Some may be viewed at home.

This medium has opened up new and splendid opportunities for better management-employee relations. Items may include people doing their jobs, which may be enlightening to other employees and up through the ranks of management to the CEO himself. Conversely, management can be introduced visually and vocally to employees who may never have met the CEO or other members of top management, With one company which operated in 50 countries this proved very effective when a new CEO was appointed and was quickly made known to everyone. Company reports and accounts have also been explained very effectively to staff, using video with perhaps a well-known TV personality interviewing the CEO.

Another interesting development has been the electronic newspaper, the pioneer being ICL with their *ICL News* produced on television screens by means of Prestel and the Baric computer. Pages can be stored for a number of days, new pages can be added daily, and employees can use Prestel-fitted television receivers at numerous company offices and factories to call up the pages they wish to read on the screen.

Documentary Films

With the added advantage that film can be transferred to videotape and vice versa, the 16mm film has, in spite of its bulky reels and the development of video, retained its popularity for a number of reasons. Chief among these is that film deteriorates less quickly than a tape, but also because 16mm film projectors exist in most places and all over the world. Although there has been rapid growth in the ownership of VCRs, they are not as common as 16mm film projectors. There are several video formats such as Sony Umatic, VHS, Betamax, Philips and others so that one has to possess a compatible VCR. And, of course, while film can be shown on large screens before large audiences, video is limited to television set screens, or larger screens which are not always available, so that it is more suitable for smaller audiences.

However, film production does lack the intricate design tricks and computerised effects which can be applied to video. Nevertheless, the

16mm documentary or industrial PR film survives, and is likely to do so for a long time to come.

Documentaries can be used for numerous purposes which justify their cost. They can be shown to invited audiences, used on exhibition stands, shown to new recruits during induction sessions, used as part of the programme at press receptions, road-showed and screened to regular audiences of clubs, societies and women's organisations, placed in libraries for lending or hiring out on request, shown in schools, distributed overseas and especially to foreign telelvision by the COI. If on 35mm stock, and of sufficient popular interest, documentaries can be shown in public cinemas as second features. There are also possibilities of use in television programmes.

The cost of making a film will depend on the number and location of outside sequences, the use of professional actors or commentators, whether special music has to be composed, and other production expenses. If a film is made to work hard, and not just allowed to rest in a library awaiting requests, it can be a valuable PR tool. Unless it contains shots which date it quickly, a film can be usable for a number of years so that the initial cost of the film, prints and servicing of the prints can be spread over these years. They can also have archival value.

A film should not be made just because someone thinks the company ought to make a film. There should be a clear purpose for the film as part of the PR strategy to use the medium to reach certain publics in order to achieve set objectives. A good film is aimed at a precise audience. As such, the documentary film is one of the most effective and most used forms of created media in the PR armoury.

Slides

The magic lantern is one of the oldest forms of visual communication, but today slide presentations range from simple showings of slides on a single projector, the Kodak Carousel being standard equipment world-wide, to sophisticated multi-screen presentations using a computerised bank of projectors. Versatility has become the hallmark of the humble slide.

Slide presentations can be coupled with audio cassettes and synchronised so that the commentary follows the sequence of slides, and the progress of the slides and commentary can be halted and re-continued as required during a presentation. Some projectors take both slides and audio cassettes or separate projector and tape recorder can be used. Another method, but one which requires twin projectors, is to make slide presentations with cross-fade effect so that there is no gap between the slides. Slides can also be put on film or videotape, an economic way of producing a film or videotape which is actually a sequence of stills.

Slide presentations have the advantage of portability, especially if standard top-loading carousel projectors are available, and made-up programmes can be carried in carousels. In this way, slide presentations can be carried anywhere, even abroad since a carousel of 80 slides or even a small box of slides is light-weight. Another advantage is that it is easy to replace slides or add to the programme.

The medium lends itself to press receptions, induction sessions, staff meetings, sales conferences, seminars and conferences - whether to a small group or to a large conference audience. The slides can be normal 35mm colour photographs, or charts, tables and headings for talks can be produced by studios which specialise in the work. Such simple visual aids enhance presentations, and are better than using blackboards, white boards or flip over charts. When management travel abroad and have opportunities to make presentations to clients it is easy to pack a made-up carousel or a box of slides.

Printed Literature

Here we mean information or educational literature as distinct from sales literature. It can be in leaflet, folder, broadsheet, brochure or book form, and may also include posters, wall-charts, calendars, picture postcards, diaries, and reprints of PR articles.

All this material can be distributed on request, used in showrooms and on exhibition stands, supplied to distributors, put in project packs for schools, issued as induction material, sent to customers and so on according to its nature and purpose.

A special kind of PR print is the sponsored publication such as a road-map, tourist guide, cookery book, gardening annual, do-it-yourself guide or sports annual. A number of these are actually sold in bookshops to mention only those of Michelin, Guinness and Rothman. Some, like McDougalls cookery book, can be advertised on the pack, while others may be offered in advertisements.

From a marketing point of view, these publications can provide admirable PR support since they encourage readers to:

(a) Use the product correctly and so obtain maximum benefit. This in turn can help to reduce complaints or queries, which could be an important PR objective in itself.

(b) Make wider use of the product, perhaps in ways or for purposes of which the customer was not previously aware. This can increase both customer satisfaction and sales.

(c) Remember the company or product, and so encourage repeat purchases.

(d) Purchase other products in the range, as in the case of accessories.

(e) Recommend the product or service to other people.

In addition, PR publications create goodwill towards the sponsor.

Even posters produced for advertising purposes can have PR value. Some, like Guinness posters, have their collectors. Many airline and tourist posters decorate the walls of clubs, canteens and other retail outlets.

Wall charts, describing various industries, are frequently displayed in classrooms, and some industries like gas and electricity produce literature especially for schools. Whereas one would not advertise to school-children, PR material is a means of educating tomorrow's market, and of reaching this particular public which could be an important one in the overall PR strategy. Also, children tell their parents and so a larger audience can be reached.

Audio Cassettes

This is an effective and economical medium since many people have tape recorders at home or cassette players in their cars. The cassette can be played and re-played, and perhaps listened to by a number of people at the same or different times. Monotony should be avoided, and more attention is likely to be paid to a tape if there are two or more voices, with perhaps the variety of a man's and a woman's voice, and music and sound effects can add further variety or greater realism. Good examples are the tapes offered by Burson-Marsteller, from one of which a quotation was made in Chapter One.

One PR use of audio tapes is in the form of audio house journals issued to staff such as salesmen who can play them in their cars. Conference venues and development corporations have either mailed or advertised tapes which describe their services. We have already mentioned the use of audio tape with slide presentations. Michelin used a tape for recruiting graduates, as mentioned in Chapter Three under Recruitment. The Royal Society For the Protection of Birds has a series of tapes on bird calls, aimed at increasing interest in bird life.

They can also be used for supplying taped interviews to radio stations, something which can be very useful when business visits are made abroad. Foreign radio stations are often interested in broadcasting the views of foreign visitors. This last example could be a valuable PR exercise for management when making overseas business trips. Compact cassettes are small, light and easy to carry.

Annual Reports

These are dealt with separately from printed literature because they feature in corporate and financial PR. They provide an opportunity not only to present required information about company results but to inform the media and a number of publics about the performance and prospects of a company. In many companies their production has become the responsibility of the PRO. The presentation of simple to understand accounts, the writing of the Chairman's report, and the design, illustration, printing and distribution of the report calls for the PRO's communication skills. Annual reports have, over the years, passed through three stages. First there was the dull, accountant's version, then there was a spate of over-elaborate reports, and today there are well-produced ones with two or three annual awards being given for the best produced company reports.

The publics for an annual report and accounts can include many people apart from shareholders, to mention only city editors, investment analysts, bank managers, and people who reply to advertisements offering copies of the report. *The Observer* offers a reader service for a selection of good reports.

Seminars and Conferences

Industrial, technical and scientific products may find small or large gatherings of invited guests an appropriate method of communication. The speakers should be technical and professional experts rather than marketing, advertising or sales executives, and the event should be kept free of promotional activity and displays. Some of the media already described may be incorporated. These may be documentary films, video, slides, exhibits (including displays of photographs) and printed literature. Displays can be on portable stands.

Top management may preside over a platform consisting of designers, engineers, scientists and other company experts who can give authentic information about their subjects. Outside speakers may be included if they are relevant, such as a buyer who can give a case-history, or a college lecturer who teaches the subject.

These PR events can be organised at various levels. A 'circus' of speakers could tour the country, or local managers could give talks and film shows to local customers. The latter is often done by bank managers. Pharmaceutical companies have organised conferences at which a new drug has been introduced to doctors. Makers of building components have organised seminars for architects and builders. It may be necessary to organise separate seminars for particular groups of people, or publics, rather than invite mixed audiences.

A modern development is video-conferencing whereby the participants can be in different locations and communicate by means of video and telephone line links. This can be done in the UK through British Telecom. The first international system of video-conferencing was the Intelmet service introduced in 1983 by Inter-Continental Hotels in conjunction with COMSAT. This enables a conference to be held between London and New York via Intelstat V communication satellites, using the tele-conferencing studios at the Inter-Continental Hotels in the two cities. The participants see each other on a four foot screen while a smaller screen can transmit documents which can be printed out in moments at either end. This system offers speed of assembly, and savings in time and travel expenses which justify the cost of about £2500 an hour. The Intelmet service is being extended to other cities where there are Inter-Continental hotels.

Advertising For PR Purposes

When it is necessary to publish exact information where and when one wants it the only choice is to buy advertising space or airtime. In the UK, little use is made of television for institutional or corporate advertising, except when a popular audience is required as we have from time to time with the energy industries. Most corporate advertising appears in the more intellectual newspapers and the business press. In the USA, corporate commercials are more common. However, although public relations is not a kind of advertising, advertising can be a kind of public relations medium. This seeming contradiction can be explained by describing some of the ways in which the PR practititioner may resort to advertising.

Management will be mostly familiar with corporate, prestige or institutional advertisements which seek to establish the image of a company by using artistic and literary advertisments narrating company history, achievements or the quality of its research. We have seen these high-sounding advertisements in *The Times*, *The Economist* and *Fortune*. There was a time when advertising agencies thought this was all PR was about. If they serve an objective, all well and good, but sometimes they are narcissistic.

Example of Corporate Advertising

However, in a double-page full-colour advertisement in *Campaign*[2] Ogilvy and Mather made much of their successful corporate advertising in the press and on television for Shell. They claimed 'Shell's tracking study has recorded shifts of attitude so large that they would bring tears of envy to any politician's eyes. One of our press ads drew such an enormous response that extra staff had to be employed to cope with it... Like all the best stories, ours has a moral, and it is that our present success owes much more than a little to Shell's long tradition of enlightened corporate activity.' Shell's brilliant corporate ads in the weekend colour magazines, and their 'Charlie' and 'Moonshot' corporate commercials have been outstanding.

One of the best and most successful result-orientated corporate advertising campaigns was that run for three years in the 70s by ITT to demolish the myths and misconceptions held about their company by top people in business, finance, the Civil Service and the Universities. There was nothing artistic or literary about those stark advertisements, the first one having a half page headline which read *Who The Devil Does ITT Think It Is?* In contrast, there was TI's series of amusing corporate commercials with Ronnie Corbett playing a number of characters, and they used television to address shareholders, dealers, customers and employees simultaneously.

Advocacy or Issues Advertising

Another form of corporate advertising is advocacy or issues advertising in which a company takes a stand on some controversial or topical subject such as nationalisation (or perhaps privatisation), taxation or proposed or contested legislation. This may be quite justified and legitimate, but it could border on propaganda if there are party political implications.

For instance, if a company subscribes to the funds of the Conservative Party and objects to the policies of the Labour Party or a Labour Government, such advocacy advertising would be propaganda rather than public relations. The difference lies in the bias. Propaganda also enters into employer sponsored advertisements during an industrial dispute. But it would be fair PR to advocate the abolition of VAT, government protection against dumping by foreign manufacturers, or the wider adoption of metrication, all of which concern people of all political persuasions.

Company Results

Advertisement space may also be taken to not just announce company results (which is normal financial advertising) but to go further and give a digest of the chairman's report and invite readers to apply for a copy of the annual report. Since the annual report has become very much a PR exercise, this kind of advertisement is a means of effecting distribution.

Co-operative Advertising

Co-operative or generic advertising is conducted by trade associations, usually funded by a levy on members, to make known the merits of, say, bricks, concrete or glass, and over the years there have been campaigns addressed to specific publics such as the Brick is Beautiful campaign or those of the publicity councils for fruit, milk, butter, cheese and eggs.

Other Uses of Advertising

Sponsorships may involve special advertising quite apart from the banners and arena advertisements which are displayed during sponsored events. For instance, several companies make awards to journalists, and space is taken to announce these awards or the results in appropriate journals like *UK Press Gazette*. More will be said about this in the following section on Sponsorships.

Yet another use of advertising for PR purposes is when a company produces educational films and wishes to make their availability known to teachers. Advertisments are placed in the educational press such as the *Times Educational Supplement* by firms like Shell and ICI.

When it is necessary to quickly recall a product which has developed a fault, press releases will be issued, but for reasons of urgency and the necessity to give precise information, space may be bought in the press for product recall advertisements. This topic will be discussed more fully in Chapter Eight.

Thus, for a variety of reasons, advertising may be used to achieve PR results, not as an alternative to PR but as a necessary PR medium in its own right.

Sponsorships

Companies may enter into sponsorships for public relations, advertising, marketing or simply philanthropic reasons, but there should be a well defined reason and the sponsorship should be capable of attaining its objective or objectives which could be a mixture of the reasons just given.

The CEO is often responsible for deciding whether or not a company should undertake sponsorship, partly because of the cost, partly because it can be a very serious company involvement. This is a medium where the CEO can no longer disassociate himself from public relations, if he is otherwise of the disdainful kind. But it is probably true that companies which indulge in sponsorships are the ones in which the CEO revels in PR. This may be because to be a sponsor a company must have arrived and so posesses a reputation which will enhance whatever it sponsors.

Why should a CEO decide to spend money on sponsorship? Sometimes it is sympathy with a certain art or sport which entices a CEO to persuade his board to support it. Before the massive support given to Test cricket by Cornhill it was ironically the American firm Gillette which rescued British county cricket from the doldrums, while Haig Whisky helped club cricket. More objectively, the Midland Bank, which has long specialised in financing agriculture, saw local show-jumping as an approach to farmers by sponsoring the sport of their sons and daughters. Again, the cigarette manufacturers are banned from television advertising but their sponsorship of golf, motor racing and other activities brings them to the television screen through coverage of events on both BBC and ITV. Coca-Cola, with its predominantly youthful market, associates itself with young people's sports such as football, athletics and swimming and does so on a world scale. Brewers from Whitbread on have backed horse racing as have bookmakers like Coral and Mecca. There is a lot of sense in being seen where your customers are plentiful. The *Sun* fully exploited its sponsorship of the Grand National, doing so daily in its racing section.

The last remarks indicate that management should be wary of sponsorships which are obscure and unrelated to their business. Nevertheless, the commercial sponsor today plays the role of the patron of old who supported artists and composers who might not otherwise be regarded today as masters. It is a responsible role, often giving great personal satisfaction and contributing to the quality of life. But for sponsorship, many pursuits would not survive or their standards would not be improved.

Sponsorship has become very big business and international events depend on the massive generosity of or investment by sponsors.

The 1984 Olympics in Los Angeles is a good example. According to *The Economist*[3], 'After television, the chief source of revenue for all modern Olympics, corporate sponsorship ranks as the most bountiful provider this time ($130m). Three dozen business giants of the General Motors, IBM and Coca-Cola ilk have elected to pour a minimum of $4m each into the games in return for the right to make advertising capital of their sponsorship. Except for a ban on direct publicity at Olympic competition events, the promotional field is wide open. Levi Strauss, the San Francisco-based jeans maker, is committing $50m, which includes giving the clothing for the American team and everybody officiating at the games - 50,000 people in all.'

What Sponsorship Can Achieve

As a public relations tool, sponsorship can achieve the following:

(a) Familiarise publics with a name.

(b) Create goodwill towards a company.

(c) Contribute to the company image since it is evidence of its behaviour.

(d) Position the company in its market.

(e) Show that the company is socially responsible.

(f) Establish recognition and acceptance of a company in a foreign market.

These are all results which contribute to a healthy environment in which the company can pursue its business.

Categories of Sponsorship

An analysis of the categories of sponsorship is as follows:

(a) *Sports.* Almost any sport one can think of has its sponsors. The principal ones are the many forms of motor sport, football, cricket, horse racing, golf, tennis, greyhound racing, show jumping, power boat racing, yacht racing, basketball, swimming, snooker, darts and table-tennis. Some are international with firms like Cadbury-Schweppes sponsoring table-tennis championships held in different countries like Nigeria with China as one of the leading contestants.

To quote Barrie Gill[4], chairman, CSS Promotions who organise sponsorships, 'The latest estimates indicate that at least £60 million will be spent by some 850 companies on sponsorship of events, competitions, personalities and teams this year. And this is a year when the British economy has hardly been booming. Even more surprising is the range of companies that have seen sport as the platform to boost their products and their corporate image. They range from cigarettes to cassettes, model cars to motor accessories, Hi-Fi to aftershave, Martini to milk, beer to insurance, carpets to tiles.'

Sponsorship does not rest with financing a sports event, team or individual, and there are accompanying functions which require the CEO's participation. He may be called upon to present prizes, and some events are opportunities to play host to parties of guests. The socialising side should not be overlooked. This should be considered in terms of cost, and additional benefits or responsibilities. The cost of hospitality may equal that of the basic sponsorship. On the other hand, the opportunity to entertain business friends and customers may be a primary objective and so justify the entire expenditure.

(b) *Arts.* In Britain, sponsorships of the arts has been encouraged by the Association for Business Sponsorship of the Arts of Bath which places emphasis on exploitation and publicity rather than mere philanthropic patronage. Subjects for sponsorship range from symphony orchestras to art exhibitions, and examples are W.D. & H.O. Wills Embassy sponsored gramophone records, Mobil Oil's provision of guide books for the Victoria and Albert Museum, and Midland Bank's promenade operas at Covent

Garden.

As Mary Allen of the ABSA explained[5] '...Mobil's art sponsorship programme was part of its corporate public relations strategy. The objective was to improve corporate awareness: to improve the recognition and respect for the company name among those who influence the business environment. The target audience was opinion leaders and decision makers. Mobil chose to sponsor the Museum because it was a respected and unambiguously British institution...'

(c) *Books.* Although this might be thought part of arts sponsorship, the sponsorship of books is more businesslike, really good ones being commercial propositions with well-known publishers putting their imprints on them, while the books are sold in the normal way. These publishing houses adopt the philosophy that there are capable authors working in industry who could write authoritative books, but to be properly illustrated and published the production costs should be shared by the employer. Thus was born the Rentokil Library of books on pest control published by Hutchinson and written by company scientists. There are also other sponsored book ventures, including the Rothman sports annuals of which their football annual has been published for many years.

(d) *Professional Awards.* Many companies make awards to professionals such as architects and photographers. However, a popular form of sponsorship which is PR-orientated is the making of annual cash awards to journalists for work which shows understanding of the sponsor's business or industry, and this may if required be limited to writers who specialise in the subject such as motoring correspondents or cookery writers.

Some well-known journalists awards are the Glenfiddich food and drink Writer of the Year, Lily Medical Journalism Research Award, the Blue Circle Awards for Industrial Journalism, the Argos Awards for Consumer Journalists, the International Building Press Journalism Awards (with various sponsors), and the Martini and Rossi's Martini Royal Photographic Competition for pictures of members of the Royal Family.

Perhaps a lesson can be learned from the Japanese who have been astute in their use of sponsorships to win friends in foreign markets, including those in South East Asia which they had occupied during the Second World War and made some very bad friends. In Britain, Japanese firms have been busy supporting popular causes in subtle ways such as Sanyo's support for British show jumper Harvey Smith, the Sanyo horses carrying distinctive blue saddle cloths which look good on television, while Britain's leading football team, Liverpool, wears jerseys sporting the name of their Japanese sponsor Sharp. Canon, who have captured British markets with cameras and, in recent years, office machines, have replaced the Football League with the Canon League. As Ken Gofton wrote in *Marketing*[6], 'What is claimed to be the biggest sports sponsorship deal so far in this country must rate as the most audacious.' But a typical Japanese take-over! Gofton also commented 'Even Canon swallowed hard when it realised how much cash it would have to find, but football - now virtually a year-round sport - was seen as the ideal sponsorship vehicle for putting the company name across to a wider public.'

British management should heed this strategy, for it is part of a world marketing strategy to place Canon at the top of the tops by 1989. With the Japanese so well entrenched in the colony, Hong Kong will not necessarily be a Chinese take-away in 1997. This recalls the message of Russell Braddon's book[7] that by 2041 Japan could become the world's supreme power, completing a century of conquest which began with Pearl Harbour. British Leyland builds Honda cars, Dunlop Holdings sells its tyre interests to Sumitomo Rubber Industries, and sponsorship may be one of the ways by which British management may retain its supremacy in fields not yet conquered by the Japanese.

Meanwhile, British management has to compete with Japanese megaprojects such as floating factories with their own floating power houses, floating international airports at £2 billion a time, or projects like the Yamberg natural gas pipeline from Siberia to Western Europe at around £20 billion. Why is a French company contracted to build the Metroline mass transit railway system in Nigeria when British firms were so successful in Hong Kong?

Sponsorships are not everything, but non-British companies are finding that sponsorship is a cost-effective way of winning recognition and status. It takes us back to the elementary task of PR to overcome hostility, prejudice, apathy and ignorance. British management could be forfeiting its renown to foreign competitors who exploit the back door of international sponsorship.

(e) *Educational.* These include academic Fellowships, bursaries, scholarships and endowments to students at universities to conduct research of value to the sponsor. New chairs at universities may also be endowed, and it was in this way that marketing first became a university degree subject. So far no-one has yet endowed a chair in public relations at a British university, although Cranfield has its MBA embracing PR.

A valuable educational sponsorship has been the sponsorship of four videocassettes by Lily on behalf of the British Diabetic Association. The cassettes are offered on loan to diabetics, and are shown on VCRs in diabetic clinics while patients are waiting to see the specialist.

(f) *Local events.* Here is an opportunity to conduct community relations by sponsoring local societies, events or causes. Local theatres have been sponsored, for example by Pilkington, and by a number of sponsors as in the case of Chichester Theatre. Complete events such as musical festivals may be sponsored, while prizes may be sponsored at flower shows.

One to One Contacts

Finally, communication between two people, eyeball-to-eyeball confrontation, can be a medium in itself whereby management actually meets opinion leaders and other individuals and misunderstandings can be dealt with face-to-face. It is surprising how antagonisms can be demolished when people actually meet and talk things over. This could be over a drink or a meal, or simply by visiting one another. Here we have public relations at its simplest and most direct.

From this survey of the macro and micro communication media

which may be used in a PR programme it will be seen that there can be a lot more to PR than press relations. Some PR programmes might never use press relations at all, e.g. one which required high level negotiations with ministers and civil servants.

REFERENCES

1. Half a Public Relations Life: Maurice Buckmaster, *Public Relations*, Longman Group, Harlow. Autumn, 1983.
2. Advertisement, Ogilvy and Mather, *Campaign*, London, April 22, 1983.
3. Olympics: Business Steps In, *The Economist*, London, September 24, 1983.
4. Gill, Barrie, Sponsorship: 1. Sport, (based on paper presented at 1982 IPR Conference), *Public Relations*, Longman Group, Harlow, Summer, 1983.
5. Allen, Mary, Sponsorship: 2. The Arts, (based on paper presented at 1982 IPR Conference), *Public Relations*, Longman Group, Harlow. Summer, 1983.
6. Gofton, Ken, Canon's Double Goal, *Marketing*, London, August 25, 1983.
7. Braddon, Russell, *The Other Hundred Years War: Japanese Bid for Supremacy 1941-2041*, Collins, London, 1983.

7.

MEDIA RELATIONS TECHNIQUES

Exposure To The Mass Media

In spite of the concluding comment in the previous chapter it is likely to be the CEO's experience that from time to time he will be either exposed to the mass media, or it is desirable that he should have direct personal relations with the press, radio and television. He may not always have the benefit of his PRO's or PR consultant's guidance or presence, and it will then be necessary for him to handle the media spontaneously and confidently. If, as is quite possible, he has inhibitions about the media, his reactions may have undesirable results. Insincerity, evasion, confusion, reticence and even shyness can be disastrous. But there is no reason why the CEO should not enjoy media relations, and be a PR asset to his company.

Let us consider his relations with each major medium in turn.

The Press

First, it is essential to understand how the press works and why, perhaps, editors and journalists may appear to be over-persistent and generally looking for the gloom and doom stories.

The best way to understand the press is to go behind the scenes and see what goes on in both an editorial office and a publisher's print shop. It could be a revelation to discover the speed with which newspapers are produced, and the deadlines which have to be met for setting, make-up, printing and distribution. Each issue of a newspaper is virtually a new product with a life cycle of little more than 24 hours in the case of a daily. Not many CEOs are concerned with such short-lived, quickly produced and consumed products.

Alternatively, a full colour women's weekly or monthly magazine has an editorial and production lead time extending over weeks or months. In Britain, publications may be printed by letterpress, offset-litho or photogravure, each having different requirements (such as quality of pictures) and different production timescales, although gradually all processes are moving over from hot metal typesetting to computerised photo-typesetting.

The press is a profession and industry unto itself, and the CEO may well find a study of it fascinating and enlightening. He will realise how easily errors creep into reports (which so many readers innocently believe to be infallible), pictures may be wrongly captioned and, above all, why the journalist's disliked persistence is due to the sheer urgency of getting the story or picture in time to edit, process and print it. In the case of a national daily, the first edition which goes on trains to the provinces is printed by 10pm while the final edition is printed by 4am. This does not allow many hours for deciding the day's policy, selecting stories and pictures coming in from all the sources listed in the previous chapter, subbing material ready for publication, and designing pages before it is ready for setting, imposition of pages, plate-making and machining followed by transportation to wholesalers who in turn have to distribute to newsagents. And then there are home deliveries with readers expecting delivery by about 7am.

If the CEO is familiar with this complex procedure he will more readily understand how to deal with the reporter who telephones him or pays him a visit, and also why the PRO or PR consultant will recommend a certain day of the week and time of a day for a press reception. Without such understanding, the CEO might insist quite unrealistically on a press reception at 6pm on a Friday evening.

When receiving a journalist the CEO should be courteous and helpful, not belligerent and un-cooperative. Not only is the journalist in a hurry but his editor has probably instructed him to get a story, and he has a job to do and keep.

The CEO is not obliged to talk to any journalist, nor is he obliged to reveal any information. But it may be in his long-term interests to do so. It may not be convenient or proper to reveal information, but this can be explained politely, and very often an alternative story can be released so that the journalist does not go away empty-handed. Sometimes it is rather like a fencing match rather than a sword fight with each daring but recognising the limits of the action.

Care is necessary about speaking candidly on topics not intended for publication, and it is wise to avoid giving information 'in confidence' or 'off the record'. Later on, back at his typewriter, it may be very difficult for the journalist to decide what was told him in confidence, or he may not regard as being confidential interesting facts which make a good story.

It is also necessary for the CEO to understand that, unless he or she is a specialist in a subject and has technical knowledge, the average journalist has to deal with a multitude of topics on which he or she has probably no previous knowledge. This is how things get misreported, and it could be the CEO's fault in not explaining complicated subjects as simply as possible. The CEO will know his subject inside out, but it could be a mystery to the journalist who is confronted with it for the first time.

This is an experience which sometimes surprises CEOs at press receptions. The CEO delivers a well-prepared speech introducing, say, a new technical product, and then from the floor come what seem to him to be stupid questions. He is disgusted by the inability of the journalists present to understand what he has just told them. But for those journalists, who may not be familiar with the technology and its jargon, it is their introduction to a subject which the CEO has been close to for a long time. One solution may be for the speaker to be supported by visual aids which help to demonstrate what he is talking about. These may be slides, charts on large boards, a prepared flip-chart or video.

Press Events

There can be three kinds of press gathering, and the CEO's role can be slightly different in each case. There is the press conference at which a statement may be made to journalists who have been called at short notice, and the hospitality is minimal. The press conference is a more simple affair then a press reception which, as the name implies, is a more organised social occasion. The press reception is planned some time in advance. It will have a programme (announced on the invitation card) which may consist of reception, speech by the CEO, demonstration, questions, and perhaps a film or video show followed by a buffet. There will be a bar and, if it is a morning event, the function will close with a cold buffet and coffee. The third kind of press event will be a facility visit to the factory or some other outside venue involving transportation of the guests, and possibly overnight accommodation and meals.

At the press conference, the CEO is the 'star of the show', and he has to make the statement and answer all the questions.

At the press reception, he is part of the programme and may not be the only speaker.

At the facility visit he is the welcoming host.

But on all occasions the CEO should never address journalists unless he has anticipated the likely questions, and is well prepared with the answers. His PR adviser can help him here by collecting up-to-date information so that the CEO is saved from embarrassment. Much depends on the style of the CEO. Some people can carry off situations when awkward questions are asked, either because they are always well-informed and articulate or because they have self-confidence and a sense of humour. Either way, they must command the situation, and not become flustered and made to look foolish. Nor must they adopt an abusive or superior tone if nettled by a difficult question. Journalists may at times seem impertinent, but it is their job to probe for facts, while the CEO retains the power and the privilege to tell or not to tell what they want to know. He has a perfect right to say 'I am sorry, gentlemen, but for the time being I am unable to answer that question.'

There is sometimes a mistaken idea that the freedom of the press means that it has a duty to its readers to tell them everything. That is nonsense. The freedom of the press means that it has the right to report freely provided it does not offend the law or good taste. Its duty is to make a profit for its owner or shareholders. Not everyone can afford to own *The Times* as a fortune wasting hobby, as the late Lord Thomson's heir refused to do. It was the late Lord Thomson who referred to his stake in Scottish Television as a 'licence to print money.' Even the present owners of *The Times*, under Rupert Murdoch's direction, introduced cost savings in 1982-3 to reduce losses from £15 million to £9 million, which were cushioned by the £36.1 million profit made mainly by the *Sun* and the *News of the World*.

News Releases

A contentious issue between management and PR practitioners is the content and wording of news releases. A further contentious issue is between companies and journalists who sometimes criticise news releases for being selective in what they say.

Very serious problems lie in these two issues, and it depends on management's willingness to accept the PR practitioner's professional advice whether or not a story will even be considered for publication by an editor. The PR man or woman should be accepted as a professional, and management should take their advice as they would from any other professional adviser. In this respect, all directors and managers concerned with the approval of a news release should understand the difference between what they would like to see in print and what an editor is prepared to print, and consequently why the PR practitioner has written the release in a certain way. Not to understand this is to kill a story, and it would be more sensible for the PR practitioner to put it in his own waste paper bin instead of helping editors to fill theirs. Every morning editors everywhere discard up to 80% of the news releases they receive because they are unprintable. Who makes them unprintable? Very often, management!

Unfortunately, various managers think they can either write releases or can write them better than the PR practitioner. It is like saying everyone can treat themselves better than their doctor, design an office block better than their architect, or plead in court better than their counsel. The worst culprits are CEOs, company secretaries and marketing managers, especially the latter. While one expects the CEO to appreciate public relations, marketing people, as noted in Chapter Two, show a curious antipathy towards PR as if it is some blasphemous interloper.

The Publishable News Release

Here is a list of the requirements of a publishable news release, with examples of how a good release can be rendered useless:

(a) The criterion of a good news release is that it must be of interest and value to the reader, and the editor is the judge of that. Many of the releases which get spiked are of interest only to the sender.

(b) The two essentials concerning the literary style of a news release are that the subject should be in the first few words, and the opening paragraph should summarise the whole story. It is rare that the company name is the subject, yet many releases start with 'The ABC Company Limited announces that...' It is journalistic style to put company names at the end of a sentence. Company secretaries may insist on the full legal name being stated but the press will usually refer to, say, Ford, Cadbury, Guinness or Dunlop. The subject is usually what has happened or will happen, e.g. 'A new transatlantic route is announced by British Airways.'

All this can be seen by simply reading the opening paragraphs in any newspaper. By reading only the first paragraphs of each report the reader can obtain a complete digest of the news. So, if only the first paragraph of a news release is printed the message will have been published.

This applies only to news releases. The story is not 'blown' in the opening paragraph of a feature article which requires an entirely different literary style. Here, the opening paragraph should capture the reader's curiosity and urge him to read on. An article is not a long news release, but an entirely different literary form.

(c) Publishing houses have their own rules about presentation, and printing practice is different from secretarial. All but the first (but sometimes all) paragraphs are indented, and block paragraphs (as in business letters) are not used. Nothing should be underlined, because this is an instruction to set in italics. Numbers should be spelt out one to nine and thereafter presented in figures except when it is clearer to say £5 million. Dates are printed month first, e.g. December 31, 1984. Capital letters are restricted to proper nouns, geographical place names, and titles like Queen Elizabeth, President Reagan, Prime Minister, Archbishop or General, but not director general, chairman, managing director or marketing manager. Business titles are reduced to small letters, even in the *Financial Times*. Abbreviations are printed without full stops, e.g. IBM and not I.B.M.

Sometimes a draft news release is re-typed by the CEO's secretary who, being unfamiliar with printing practice, will introduce her quite different secretarial style. Before the release is fit to be sent out, the PRO or PR consultant has to correct all these errors. If he does not the editor will think him an amateur, and it means a lot of unnecessary editorial corrections. The credibility of a news release could be marred by its incredible and unprofessional appearance.

(d) A news release must contain no 'puffery' which is the editor's name for advertising, and editors hate advertising. Puffery consists of superlatives, comment and self-praise. The story should consist of facts, not advertisement copy, nor opinions which the editor may not share. In other words, a release should read like a typical newspaper report, as if a journalist had written it given the same facts. No greater accolade could be given a news release than to have it printed word for word as written and by-lined with a journalist's name. Marketing managers are apt to criticise news releases because they do not boost a company or product sufficiently, but it is not an advertisement and journalistic writing is quite different from copywriting. Nor are clever headlines necessary since each editor will compose his own headline, probably to fit the space.

The above descriptions of news release writing techniques are given to help management to understand why a news release has been written in a certain way, and why managerial interference could destroy its chances of being published. But management loves to tinker with releases! It is a case of keeping a dog and barking oneself.

Exhibitions

Management can play an important PR role at exhibitions, the CEO being present on the stand on press day and at the official opening when he can meet the press and welcome the official opener if he or she visits the stand. Trade exhibitions can be a PR gesture when customers can meet management, and at both public and trade exhibitions receptions can be held on the stand for special guests with the CEO as host.

Television

The characteristics, opportunities and snares of television have been analysed in Chapters Five and Six but here let us touch on three aspects which particularly concern the CEO if he is to appear 'on the box.'

Three Aspects of Television

(a) Time. Television production can be very time consuming and may involve a lot of technicians who have to be accommodated, although with portable video cameras this will be less so. But usually, a special day and time has to be arranged. If the televising is connected with a press reception, filming will probably take place on a different day in a different place. Although the result may be only a few minutes or less on the screen, half a day may be taken up in producing it, and this will include two or three dummy runs before the actual interview is shot. A studio interview is also time consuming since one has to travel to the studio, and go through preliminaries which may include a little make-up before the live interview occurs. Screen time will be brief, and the subject may think he has been dealt with very abruptly when the cameras are finally on.

(b) Appearance. Being a visual medium, viewers will be very critical of what they see on the screen. They will notice physical oddities or peculiarities or attractiveness of dress. These in themselves could be attractions. The hair style, spiky eyebrows, style of spectacles, shape of ears, nose, chin or mouth, moustache or beard will all be distinctive visual elements. The more interesting - rather than handsome or beautiful - the subject looks the better. The person interviewed should look credible because in a sense he is an actor playing his own role. Does he look as if you can believe what he says?

This is where the PR practitioner has to intervene and either suggest that the CEO does not appear on television, or some other senior company spokesman does. There are CEOs who look like undertakers. It may be advisable to attend a TV training course.

It must also be remembered that television is in colour, and it may be worth observing how attractively newcasters and presenters dress. Without destroying credibility, it will be better to wear a blue or brown suit rather than a black one, and to pick a nice tie with a touch of colour in it. Red is a colour which is often missing from colour pictures, and this can be a contrasting colour to use. Possibly, a pink shirt, a red motif on a tie or red hair may make the contrast!

(c) Speech. It is necessary for the company spokesman to be confident and fluent. He must not be surprised if he is not allowed to say what he would like to say, and he may feel like a witness being cross-examined by an aggressive counsel. Nor must he be floored by the unexpected question. He may be put off by the busyness of a studio and the heat of the lights, but he should try to concentrate on the interviewer and ignore all the studio apparatus of cameras, lights and their technicians. Television studios can be overwhelming, seemingly untidy places with a lot of disconcerting action taking place.

When being interviewed, it is best to make oneself as relaxed as possible, settling comfortably into the chair so that one does not fidget afterwards or sit too rigidly. Composure is very important. The witness box feeling should be overcome so that smiles, gestures and replies come spontaneously. One should not try to bully the interviewer in Margaret Thatcher fashion, but neither should one be defensive and apologetic. Confidence comes from knowing what one is talking about, but care is necessary not to introduce too many figures or statistics because they are difficult for viewers to absorb orally.

Radio

Here we have an entirely different medium. A radio interview almost resembles a telephone conversation, with both the interviewer and the audience being like the person at the other end of the line.

Radio is far less inhibiting than television because, as suggested above, it is more like a conversation. It will be conducted in a room, office, small studio, or possibly out-of-doors. The only visible equipment in a studio is a microphone and perhaps a tape recorder. In the studio the guest will probably be unaware of the engineer behind his glass window. The whole interview, including a preliminary chat or rehearsal, may take only twenty minutes.

For radio interviews it is easier to relax and talk naturally, but again it is necessary to be well-briefed and capable of responding to questions instantly and fluently. The television interview may be hurried - television air time is always scarce - but radio occupies far more air-time and - partly because of the lack of visual effects - the pace of an interview is more gentle. It therefore pays to speak more slowly, and there will be less pressure to keep to time limits. Even so, the radio interview will occupy only a few minutes so answers need to be succinct and free of hesitations.

Whereas appearance is important on television it is the voice which has to be interesting on radio. Regional accents can be attractive, and so can the occasional good-natured chuckle. With this medium we are communicating by means of sound, and it is the listener's ear as well as mind which has to be pleased. An interesting looking person on television may be forgiven if he speaks poorly, but how a person sounds is all-important on radio. Oratory is not wanted, but sincerity is essential. To test one's ability to come over well on radio it is a good idea to use a tape recorder and test the sound of one's own voice. The playback is likely to reveal one startling thing: one's own voice sounds different to other people from what it sounds to oneself when speaking. Not many people are actually familiar with the sound of their own voice.

8.

SPECIAL ACTION AREAS OF MODERN PUBLIC RELATIONS

Management may regard the PR practitioner as an oracle capable of achieving the impossible, and demands made upon PROs and PR practitioners are often surprising. It may help the status of the PR practitioner to retain this legend, but the wise PR man or woman is humble enough to adopt the philosophy that every day is a new day. The most fascinating characteristic of PR is that one is always learning, that one never knows it all although constantly asked to give expert advice, for it is a problem solving business. The greatest attribute in PR is the ability to find out.

Consequently, there is nothing static about PR, and the PR practitioner has to be capable of satisfying the demands of today's fast changing world. In this chapter futuristic prophesies will not be indulged for the pattern of the next twenty years is already emerging if not apparent. Management can no longer afford to distance itself from PR because PR has become entwined in management decisions. As seen in the discussion on tangible PR and the outline of some forty possible PR objectives in Chapter Two, the range of PR activity has become enormous. We have moved a long way from the world of press relations, important though that may still be, and in this chapter certain special areas of modern public relations will be looked at more closely. These developments concern both in-house PR and consultancy PR, both of which have responded to the special needs of the recession and the birth of the post-industrial era.

Crisis PR

Crisis or disaster PR consists of the readiness to deal with the communications problems provoked by an emergency situation. For any company there can be a number of emergency situations which could erupt. The trick is to recognise their possibility, not ignore them because such calamities have never happened. This can be a sobering revelation for the leadership of a business which does not seem to be vulnerable. The 'it won't happen to me' attitude could be foolhardy optimism.

The more obvious disasters are strikes, fires, explosions, accidents and financial ones such as losses or take-over bids. But there can be many temporary, unforeseen disasters such as a product failure, some deficiency over which the company has no control, or a totally unexpected horror situation when an apparently well-tested and reliable product has produced dangerous side effects.

We have had product failures in electrical or electronic goods containing imported components; famous foods, restaurants and hotels have been condemmed for unhygienic products causing illness and in some cases deaths; while a number of pharmaceuticals have been withdrawn from the market following their fatal or ill effects on patients or their off-spring. No-one will forget the Thalidomide disaster, and every drug company dreads such a disaster, and a more recent one concerned a product for the treatment of arthritis. In a world of wonders we face unpredictable terrors which can harm the reputation and sales of the most reputable company.

They cannot be glossed over. Crude white-washing is impossible. It is true that the higher you climb, the further you fall. The old idea that a PRO could be hired to pretend it had never happened has long since died the death it deserved. PRO's are not troubleshooters. Modern, instant news media, intensified by satellites, has taken care of that.

Fortunately for management - and this is not meant to be cynical or any attempt to evade responsibility - two things do operate favourably. Most of these disasters have happened before, however rare they may be, but even a nine-day wonder has to be handled properly. The public memory is short, and the disaster may well be forgotten in time, but there is still the present to deal with. So, while with luck and patience there may be these two compensations, the current situation still has its problems and dangers.

It is also true, and this is important, that the manner in which an unfavourable situation is handled can be to the credit of a company. Out of adversity can be created goodwill. When a cruise liner was unable to allow its passengers ashore because of an outbreak of illness on board, the efforts to placate the unfortunate passengers were so good that many of the passengers booked for other cruises by the same line the following year.

Let us take an everyday example. A complaint from a customer is bad news for the supplier. If he acts defensively, he makes an enemy, but if he is apologetic, obliging and converts the complaint into praise, he has made a friend. In a simple way, this sort of thing can be management policy, understood throughout the company in readiness for eventualities.

One is reminded of the time-honoured story of the owner of a Rolls-Royce which broke down during a holiday trip in Spain. Engineers were immediately flown out and the car was repaired. On his return to England, the owner telephoned Rolls-Royce to express his thanks. He was told the company had no record of the breakdown; in fact their motor-cars did not break down! Perhaps that is the ultimate in crisis PR. Normally, it is impossible to get away with a denial.

The Cost of Recall

Product recalls can be costly from the replacement point of view, but they can also be costly in goodwill if they are conducted clumsily. In a country as large as the USA it may be very difficult to trace quantities of a faulty product, and prohibitively costly to use media advertising. Corning Glass mounted a classic PR campaign in the USA to recover coffee pots which shed their handles, described in another book[1] by the author, but nevertheless the recall cost $17m.

Further examples were given in an article in the *Financial Times*[2]. The John West canned salmon recall cost £2m, a Remington razor recall cost £500,000, the recall of 7.5m Firestone tyres cost $150m, while the French company Kleber is said to have lost $6m in sales because they refused to recall suspect tyres. Such stories are headline hoggers.

It does not stop there. In magazines like Lloyd's monthly *Product Liability*, unsafe products are reported. There is the 'hot line' system in American newspapers which seek to protect the public, while British newspapers are quick to expose dangerous products, the British Safety Council is devoted to this task, and television documentaries and popular series like Esther Rantzen's *That's Life* give unfavourable publicity to rogue companies, products and services.

In the majority of cases, there is never any intention to foist a bad product on an unsuspecting public and profit from the deception. The defect is often a freak accident. However, it can sometimes disclose a situation unsuspected by customers. Until the deaths from botulism and the scare which followed, one might have supposed from the John West advertising, which made certain claims about the quality of the salmon, that it was actually packed by them, not that they labelled or had labelled cans packed overseas.

Howard Abbott in his *Product Recall Management Guide*[3] makes these comments: 'It is a fact of life that any company that makes products in large numbers will get it wrong at least once, even though the product may conform to well-known standards, be approved by prestigious bodies and have been subjected to stringent quality tests. Even the great and the good get caught.' By way of describing some of the difficulties involved when a recall is necessary, Abbott comments: 'Many companies have no systematic forward distribution plan because their sales network has evolved gradually over a period of time. In such circumstances, to try to put the distribution system into reverse can lead to chaos.'

Even more in context with the theme of this book is Abbott's two-fold advice on how to be prepared to deal spontaneously with a product recall. He says 'When reports of a product defect start coming in a decision will have to be taken on its possible consequences. To do this requires completely accurate knowledge of the details of the product out in the market place .... Once a dangerous product defect has been confirmed the company must be able to identify exactly which units or production batches are involved. To do this an effective system of product "finger printing" must be in force, for this is not something that can be done retrospectively, it has to be in operation continuously.'

There may also be occasions when there is doubt about whether a malfunction actually exists, and it can help if satisfied customers are willing to express their continued confidence in the product. This could be important with industrial products where the fortunes of other businesses using the product are jeopardised by the complaints and the resultant bad publicity. Such a case occurred when aircraft were grounded world-wide following the crash of a DC-10 in France, and it may be recalled how Sir Freddie Laker, whose Laker Airways flew the aircraft, made public statements on television that he had complete faith in the machine.

Bad Publicity

Widespread publicity can help a product recall, and this can be a mixture of press relations and press advertising, but the popular press may dramatise such news. For instance, the *Sun*[4] (with a sale of more than four million copies) ran two crisis stories above each other in the same column with the following headlines:

Danger!
Killer
plugs
peril on
washday

and

COCKROACH
CHARGE IS
KICKED OUT

The first was to do with Italian plugs attached to spin dryers, the second about a summons against a famous London restaurant, the proceedings (and all the unhygienic details) having been reported on previous days. In the latter case, the dismissal of charges could not undo the bad publicity that had already appeared, naming not only the restaurant but the big hotel group to which it belonged.

Crisis Management

Robert Slater[5], vice-president, Manning, Selvage & Lee Inc, the American PR counsellors, says 'there are two kinds of public relations crises that can happen: known unknowns, or unknown unknowns.' The first consist of products or industries where risk is possible. The subject is known but what will go wrong is unknown until it happens. For instance, an airline could have a crash, but it cannot be anticipated how, when or where it will happen. Or it could be a personal issue: supposing the chairman dies? Unknown unknowns are beyond prediction. It is possible to anticipate that a hotel may suffer a fire, even that guests could die from food poisoning, which are unknown hazards of the industry, but one cannot anticipate the assassination of a Presidential guest with all its abundant international news coverage.

Three advance actions are recommended by Slater:

'1. Take steps to prevent a disaster before it occurs.
2. Establish standby measures should an emergency happen.
3. Design a program to recoup your company's good name.'

It takes both courage and foresight for management to recognise that a disaster is possible. Some disasters may not seem feasible until they happen, like the Great Train Robbery, the mass escape of prisoners from the Maze in Belfast, or the shooting down of the Korean airliner by the Russians. Slater says: '...make a list of known unknowns. Every time you hear or read about a disaster happening to another company, add it to your list. Decide whether or not it is a known unknown for your company - and if it is, plan for it and make your company plan for it.'

Obviously, it is good PR for management to be wise before the event, and this may actually identify risks which can be eliminated altogether so that reputation and goodwill are not endangered. Sensible preventive action is always preferable, and a simple example of this is to write warnings into instructions. It is all very well assuming that people will not use products dangerously, but there is always the possibility that they will. For instance, warnings on pesticides that they should be kept out of the reach of children and animals must have avoided a great many tragedies, but not everyone reads warnings. What happens when there is no antidote? This haunted one manufacturer, and a twin crisis on the same day actually struck the company. Such were the subsequent successes of the company that the incident is now forgotten.

Handling The Press

When the bad day occurs, press, radio and television will be on the doorstep. What do you do? The media may be sympathetic as when the *Queen Elizabeth II*, packed with journalists, broke down on its maiden voyage. The PRO came out of a shower with a towel wrapped round him to explain to the world by radio telephone what had happened. But the whole media could be unsympathetic because cows and dogs had died, and they hounded the company at three different addresses for weeks in the case of the product without an antidote mentioned above.

Vivian Manuel[6], president of VM Communications of New York, points out that while 'nobody wins in a crisis situation' it is possible that 'some do's and don'ts can make a difference between a tie score and a defeat in your dealings with the media.'

He sets out the following criteria: '...make sure that your top management is fully aware of the crisis and is committed to giving full attention to the need for handling press enquiries....Assign one person the responsibility for responding to the media.... Be there; be available....Know what you are talking about....Respond to *every media query. Return all* phone calls...Don't lie. Reporters are like elephants - they never forget....But don't say more than you have to....Don't use business jargon....Don't get prematurely committed to the public announcement of a company policy or position in a crisis situation....Don't lose your cool - regardless of the question or the reporter's attitude.....Don't - *ever* - ask for favors from the media in a crisis situation ....If the crisis involves more than one company....or more than one segment of a single company....be sure you have a "command communication centre" set up....keep top management informed, in writing if possible, about which reporters you've talked to and what you have said to them.'

The above quotation is a digest of Vivian Manuel's do's and don'ts, and although they are addressed to members of the International Association of Business Communicators, they also tell management a lot about the responsible behaviour to be expected from the in-house PRO. It is also typical of the practical approach to business communications which one finds in the IABC.

Essential Stages of Crisis PR

From the selection of professional advice given above it will be seen that crisis PR has become an essential action area in modern public relations. Every few days one reads or hears of a product recall, no doubt because sophisticated products are seldom perfect but frequently because the battle against inflation has led to more economical purchasing, often from abroad, that has overridden the exacting quality control of more expensive components or materials.

Double problems occur when a tanker disaster causes oil slicks which pollute the beaches of holiday resorts; all a company's famous drugs are in peril when one is found to have horrendous effects on patients; communities fear for their health and safety when there are explosions, escapes of toxic materials, or foul effluents from factories; transportation firms lose goodwill and passengers when there are crashes or breakdowns; not only profit on current sales but profits on future sales disappear when strikes oblige or encourage customers to buy elsewhere; companies with falling share prices, and others apparently less vulnerable but with powerful competitors, face take-over bids; and natural disasters like earthquake, famine and floods cause crises for governments and fund-raising charities. All these happenings have been commonplace in modern life, heightened in impact by the huge number of people and the high cost of disasters which make them nationally and often internationally newsworthy.

They are management nightmares. From the PR point of view, they are crises of confidence. Once again we are back to negative states of hostility, apathy, prejudice and ignorance. Knowledge is required to create or re-create understanding. Confidence, goodwill and reputation depend on it. It is a supreme test for PR. The situation is unfavourable, and nothing can change that, although it is just possible that people will admire or respect a company's behaviour in dealing with the situation. It may be necessary to 'climb down the greasy pole', and start all over again. One can always 'live to fight another day'.

The following procedures can now be deduced as a practical way to prepare for and handle crisis situations. These are now well-established in large organisations which have faced up to possible perils, but management in many more companies could adopt such a plan.

1. *Anticipate and rehearse possible disaster situations.* Slater[7] says make a list of known unknowns. Do more than this. Borrow from the Mexican Statement which says analyse trends and anticipate consequences. Crisis PR is in itself a case of the Mexican Statement formula being applied to one special programme. What are the consequences of a strike likely to mean? Contracts with transporters, dealer relations, customer relations, exhibition plans and advertising campaigns are all involved in addition to industrial relations. What is the time differential between run down of existing stock and lack of output? How long can a strike be sustained? The logistics of entering into a strike situation are calculable, and form part of bargaining strength or weakness. But taking Slater's first advance action, is there yet another PR aspect of management-employee communications which could avert a strike? In Britain, a great deal of industrial action results from old-fashioned management rather than union militancy.

Strong management of the Michael Edwards style is not always good management, and there *are* companies which never have strikes. On the continent and in Japan there are competitors of strike-prone British firms which never have stikes, and not only because they have industrial rather than craft unions. A strike is usually a result of bad management-employee communications and indifferent industrial relations policy. Customers tend to look at it this way too: when their new car is delayed because of a strike, they blame the company, not the workers who are only other people like themselves. So they buy a German or Japanese car. Even today, with a certain amount of robotics, Ford in Britain still talk about 'Monday' and 'Friday' cars which do not exist in most foreign car factories.

More stringent safety precautions, including educational PR to inspire greater care, can offset accident, fire, explosion and other hazards. Nothing can be taken for granted, yet in many hotel and other fires negligence has been revealed which has marked managerial irresponsibility. How closely does management ally itself with safety, or does it rely too much on safety officers or simply on good luck? People have died simply because a door was always kept locked, and there could be a conflict between security and safety.

Some industries, such as the toy making, concern themselves with 'foreseeable misuse'. Lego[8], for instance, go to great lengths to test every aspect of their products in order to eliminate dangerous characteristics. The plastic blocks and other components are tested to see that they cannot be swallowed, fingers cannot be trapped or cut, that components cannot be broken by biting, dropping or stepping on, that the materials contain no heavy metals or soluble dyes which might be swallowed, and that the products can be washed safely.

How often are there fire drills or dummy runs on disaster prone locations? It is no use relying on visits by factory inspectors, fire brigade officers or health department inspectors. Standards should be higher than those set out in regulations. For example, cabin staff demonstrate life saving equipment before airliners take off. Very few passengers take any notice. But put this on video, as Laker Airways did, and few people can resist looking at the screen.

2. ***Set up an organisation to deal with emergencies.*** The next

stage is to set up a team of technical experts (including PR) which can go into action immediately an emergency occurs. It is no use saying there are already people in responsible positions who can deal with a crisis when it occurs. They may not succeed if they are not an integrated team rehearsed in the necessary action. It may also mean that equipment has to be available like the fire engines at airports, or the special vessels which have been built since the first oil rig disasters. In Hong Kong, for instance, government PR staff have special hurricane duties. Company staff, directed by the CEO, works managers and other location managers, need to be rehearsed periodically.

A twenty four hour press office should be ready to handle the media, with a rota of staff allocated to different periods of the day. If the normal staff is small, plans should exist for augmenting them with other personnel who can be called in quickly. They could be retired staff, freelancers or members of a PR consultancy retained and briefed for the purpose. This will depend on the kind of company and the nature of the emergency, but it would be unrealistic to expect a lone PRO to operate a twenty four hour service over an indefinite period. Disasters do not operate on a nine-to-five basis.

Moreover, as Vivian Manuel[9] pointed out in his 'do's and don'ts', the PRO is not only dealing with the media. He has to maintain lines of communication with both sources of information and top management. He has to operate output of information, feedback and be an intelligence system. He must never be regarded as a bulwark agains the press, that is, a management defence system.

3. *Action in the Event.* The team must know what to do and what not to do in the event. This does not just mean closing ranks, but taking positive action, initiating action if possible rather than allowing the media the advantage. This will be made much easier if the PRO has plenty of facts on file, and pictures too. There may be little time to collect facts, but it is not difficult to have a dossier of information about what has suffered a disaster. Being well informed at the onset makes it all the easier to issue a statement as far as circumstances permit, as soon and as frankly as possible.

There may be important strictures on what may be said. There could be legal or insurance restrictions on admitting liability, or need to notify relatives first before names of injured or dead are released.

4. *Permit Access to Media As Soon As Possible.* A natural reaction of the media, when something goes wrong, is that the organisation concerned will be defensive. The more readily the media are given access to information and, if possible, access to the scene of the disaster the more quickly will the confidence of the media be established. This needs to be organised as soon as possible. It may be necessary to provide transportation. A viewing area may be required, or a tour arranged. Hospitality will be required. Telephone facilities are necessary. It is better to take the initiative and play host than to put up barriers which only provoke the media into taking the initiative in ways which may prove irritating and offensive.

There is another aspect: A number of crisis stories have received minimal media coverage because immediate access to a story showed that there was little to report, and the story (and its bad publicity) was exhausted in a day. But had the company gone on the defensive, refusing access, making 'no comment' rejections, and virtually keeping the media at bay, the media would have gone on for days hunting for a story and probably publishing lurid speculations in the absence of facts.

5. *When The Problem Has Been Solved.* It may not be possible to issue a full statement until investigations have been completed, normal services have been resumed, or the disaster has been overcome. Then, the media should be given the complete story. The media may have to wait for this, and they will have to be treated patiently because they will persist in seeking an early story and perhaps an individual scoop. The media should be treated equally because scoops will be bad for future media relations. There should be no cover-up or suspicion of one, otherwise the media will hunt for the hidden story. The final story should be conclusive and put an end to any speculation there might have been.

The closing of a disaster is an art in itself. The story may simply die because there is no more to be said, but it may be necessary to convince the media by arranging a press visit. This is a point where the authority of the CEO will be important. He has the final say. Peace has been declared.

Coping with the unpredictable is a service offered by PR consultancies such as Burson-Marsteller who operate world-wide. This service is described in their brochure *Communication Skills*[10] in these words: 'Crisis program development begins with strategic planning meetings with key managers. Together, we consider the communication options available during a potential crisis situation. We analyze risks and benefits associated with each option and develop a crisis handling policy. We anticipate the after-effects or repercussions of actions. Should we take a pre-emptive or reactive stance? Who is affected? How will other affected individuals or groups respond?'

Management-Employee Relations

In earlier chapters the communication audit, internal relations audit and the media of upward and downward management-employee relations have been discussed. Now let us look at staff relations (as distinct from industrial relations and personnel management) as a growth area in public relations. This is both the oldest and the newest form of PR, its span stretching from the *Lowell Offering* of 1842 described by Charles Dickens in *American Notes* to the Prestel electronic newspaper, such as *ICL News* of modern times. The house journal is evidence of more than a century of internal PR. But why has management-employee relations become so important today? Why, for instance, has its growth fostered the most efficient professional body in the communication world, the International Association of Business Communicators which, like a transnational business organisation, is outstripping purely national institutes?

It is symptomatic of a changing world. The corporate dinosaurs of the industrial age are dying. As Steve Vines said in an interview[11] 'We are at the end of the age of dinosaurs, the future lies with those who have a smaller body size and are speedier to adapt.' Already, we have seen this with robotics at BL which has shed thousands of workers.

Coupled with this is the diminishing power of other dinosaurs, the trade unions, so feared by management before Britain's dole queue hit the multi-millions.

Recession has made for slimmed down industries and the arrival of smaller firms. One of Britain's most successful companies, Sinclair Research Ltd., with its home computer, flat-screen pocket TV and electric town car, employs only 60 people, although another 2000 are employed in firms which produce and market the product. It makes more profit than British Leyland, British Steel, the National Coal Board and British Shipbuilders put together - £14 million in 1982.[12]

Democratisation of industry is with us too, with employees speaking up to management, co-partnership, profit-sharing, employee share owning, and, to a lesser extent in Britain but certainly in some other countries, works committees, works councils and worker-directors.

The old class-ridden 'master and servant' system of management is disappearing. We have quality circles now in which teams of workers project ideas, incentive schemes in which workers benefit by submitting cost saving ideas, participatory independent house journals on paper, video or Prestel, plus computerised communications with VDUs and international teleconferencing by satellite. In a few brief years, communication has become easy, and where better to conduct it than within the company? The sheer ease and freedom of communication is breaking down internal communication inhibitions of the past. One of the reasons for bad management-employee communications in the past was simply that it was very difficult to talk to huge work forces. When Rentokil appointed its new managing director Clive Thompson, it was able to introduce him to employees in fifty countries by means of an interview on their video magazine, *Rentokil Roundabout*[13].

Let us consider the purpose of internal relations, what can or should be communicated, by whom and by what means.

If we take the means first, the media may consist of wall newspapers, notice boards, newsletters, magazines, newspapers, audio tapes, video, electronic newspapers, Tannoy system, in-house radio, speak-up schemes, staff meetings, works committees, works councils and so on.

Some media may have limited distribution and specialist appeal. A great mistake in old-fashioned internal communications is to imagine everyone is interested in everything, or to issue a single printed house journal which tries to be all things to all employees. But internal media have to be like external commercial media - newsletters, business newspapers, popular tabloids and so on according to reader interests. Too little attention is paid to the appropriateness of internal media. This has nothing to do with the size of a company, but it may mean that internal communication is under-budgeted. Again, a paternal attitude should not be adopted, nor should house journals and other forms of internal communication be regarded as gifts or luxuries. They are essentials of good management, investments in internal harmony.

What to communicate to whom can be placed under the three headings of upwards, sideways and downwards communication, using whatever may be the most effective media.

Upwards Communication

Under this heading come methods of communication initiated by employees in their own interests, thus reversing the paternal role of earlier management-dominated communications. But there are also some management inspired forms of upward communication, stemming from enlightened management and democratised industrial relations. Wherever possible, management should encourage upward communication.

1. *Readers Letters.* One way of attracting participation by employees is to invite readers of house journals to submit 'letters to the editor.' This does not mean that everyone is entitled to have his or her letter published, or to say what they like, because a house journal has to be produced like any commercial journal. Space is limited, the readers' letters feature requires a balance of views and topics, and in the interests of good taste abusive letters have to be rejected or toned down. But as with commercial journals, even unpublished letters help the editor and may indicate subjects which interest readers and should be covered in future issues. A letter could lead to an interview or a feature article.

2. *Interviews with readers.* The ideas, views and experiences of employees may be obtained by interviewing them. These candid interviews may be published or shot for a video magazine. This can be an interesting form of upward communication because not only will fellow employees learn about each other but management may be enlightened about what people in the organisation actually think and do.

3. *Features about employee interests.* An independent editor of a staff newspaper can take up employee problems, and analyse them objectively so that a case is made for the consideration of management. Such features may be inspired by complaints received by the editor, or the personnel manager, or unearthed by the editor as he moves about the company and talks to people. For example, the editor of *Ford News* thought there could be improvements in an incentive scheme, and published his ideas on the subject.

4. *Speak-up and Suggestion Schemes.* These are invitations to employees to communicate their ideas and recommendations to management. A system is necessary, such as printed forms and collection boxes in which written ideas are placed. This is done very well in IBM offices and factories.

5. *Open door.* Although initiated by management, the 'open door technique' permits employees to visit management to discuss problems or make suggestions. It might be thought that management would be swamped by uninvited visitors, but in practice this is seldom so. The secret of this method is the psychology of accessibility to management, and elimination of the idea that management are remote and unapproachable.

6. *Works Committees, Works Councils, other committees.* At these regular assemblies of employees, two-way communication can be established at which proposals and opinions of employees can be discussed together with company policies. Although more common on the continent than in Britain, there are British companies which operate them. Some companies have executives or middle-management

committees. They can provide safety valves that avoid disputes, and they do enable employees to have a more intimate knowledge of management policies and plans which again can reduce tensions and misunderstandings and prevent unnecessary industrial disputes. As one German trade unionist said, by knowing the financial situation in a company 'we do not kill the cow that gives the milk.' Unfortunately, some British trade unionists believe that such committees and councils usurp their negotiating rights, while some managements are impatient with the necessary proceeds. But as Philips have found in Eindhoven, works councils may slow down decision making to some extent, but they obviate strikes.

7. *Correspondents for House Journals.* Companies with many locations and employee societies can have correspondents who feed news to the editor of the employee newspaper. They provide communication links which help employees to express themselves. In their outposts, correspondents are listening agents, the eyes, ears and voices of the internal communication system.

8. *Quality Circles.* This Japanese idea, now adopted internationally, is developed in Mike Robins'[14] book but briefly it consists of regular meetings of groups of no more than ten people of similar job function, headed by their supervisor. Discussions are held which are franker more aggressive and more productive than suggestion and speak-up schemes. Quality circles should have the blessing of management which should heed the outcome of the regular meetings. Quality circles produce results such as improved worker attitudes and involvement in company affairs, reduced absenteeism (if that is a problem), and generally improved productivity.

9. *Equity Ownership.* Increasingly popular today is the sale of shares to employees, and sometimes priority sales to them of new issues. This can be a new experience since workers are often critical of shareholders. Equity ownership of shares by employees creates a new dimension in internal relations. Not only does this kind of shareholder enjoy a share in the company's prosperity, but he has a special motive for contributing to that prosperity. And as a shareholder he has a right to attend the annual general meeting, or at least vote by proxy. He has a voice in the fortunes of the company in which he works.

10. *Co-partnership.* With co-partnership, of which we have examples in Kalamazoo of Birmingham and John Lewis stores of London, we go a step further into employee participation. Like the works council, it is a form of industrial democracy which is being advocated in Britain today as a means of revitalising our old class-ridden industry. When every worker has a stake in the company for which he works, there is no place for destructive 'moles' or trade union militancy. He is no longer an isolated drone, separated from the financial ownership and the distribution of profits. He has a mutual interest. This can also encourage staff stability.

Sideways Communications

Here we have systems of communications between members of the staff, using media such as the house journal or the controlled notice board. Some examples are:

1. *Sales and Wants Advertisements.* A means of increasing reader interest in a house journal is to publish readers' sales and wants advertisements. The work force provides a market place for secondhand and other items such as houses, or for privilege price goods offered by, say, the staff horticultural society. Advertisements make a journal resemble a commercial publication, and classified advertisements make interesting reading.

2. *Communications With Other Employees.* In organisations in which staff are scattered or moving about, as in an airline or shipping company, the house journal helps employees to know where their friends are working or currently posted.

3. *News About Staff Societies.* Reports on the activities of staff clubs and societies provide members with important news, and help to build social relations between members of the staff. These are activities initiated by the staff, and the necessary communications through the house journal or controlled notice board are a form of sideways communication which is separate from management-employee relations. In Shell, for instance, news items are handed in to the PR department, and artistically produced notes are clipped to their respective positions on controlled notice boards.

Downward Communications

Having moved a long way from the paternal communications of old to acceptance of management's need to develop management-employment communications, coupled with the increasing number of facilities for doing so, here are some of the things which some managements can or should communicate.

1. *Trading results.* Interim and annual reports, results and dividends are nowadays presented through internal media such as house journals and video magazines, being printed in digest or diagramatic form, or in interviews with the CEO, so that they are intelligible to employees. It is necessary to explain how the company's income is dispersed to materials, overheads, labour, bank charges, taxation, re-investment and dividends. This has been done extremely well on film and video by Ocean Transport and Trading of Liverpool, even when the company was having bad years, while on one occasion the managing director of Rentokil was interviewed on the video magazine *Rentokil Roundabout* to explain why the company had made less profit than usual.

2. *Company Policy.* Changes or developments of company policy need to be explained so that employees understand why the company is behaving in a certain way. If this is not done, rumours can spread provoking fears and the sort of explosive situations which can lead to needless strikes. The grapevine is the worst kind of communication system.

3. *Board and Managerial Appointments and Responsibilities.* The staff need to know who is running the company, and managerial 'family tree' operational charts can demonstrate the functions. Video is very

useful here in introducing new directors and executives. This is very important with large companies, particularly international ones with many locations, in which opportunities to meet management may be rare. The more familiar the staff are with the management structure and personalities, the easier it is to create internal confidence and stability.

4. *New Products and Services.* Employees should be kept aware of the introduction of new products and services, some of which may be produced at other factories. This heightens job satisfaction and encourages pride in the company's achievements, or at least confidence in its progress. For some members of the staff, it may be essential that they are familiar with new products, packaging and prices, or understand product uses. If they are sales staff, new product features in the house journal will help them to demonstrate and sell. This can be additional to instructions and information distributed by the sales department, and will augment it.

5. *Sales Contests and Incentives.* The announcement of sales contests, awards and incentive schemes, and the names of winners, may be announced through various media such as house journals, sales bulletins, audio tapes, video magazines, posters and notice boards. Some contests may be run on a monthly 'top ten' basis with monthly and annual prizes, or bonuses or scores which can be counted towards a final award. Incentive schemes awards can be written up in detail, showing how the prize-winning idea will contribute to greater efficiency or economy, and so encourage others to submit ideas.

6. *Equity Ownership.* This is also a process of downward communication and is repeated here from the management standpoint. Employees may be invited to buy shares, or have priority when there is a new issue. The purchase of shares needs to be explained carefully to staff who are not normally shareholders. There is, for instance, a risk element which has to be understood, while the nature of share prices and dividend payments have to be clarified. Unless the facts are made clear, there could be misunderstanding and even resentment. But even among those who do not buy the company's shares the offer could create better understanding of what shareholding means, and the importance of this means of financing the company.

7. *Acquisitions, Mergers and Amalgamations.* These inevitably traumatic occasions need to be explained to employees so that they understand efforts such as the restructuring of the company, absorption of competition, extension and diversification of interests, strengthening of the company and so on. Coupled with this will be the human interest aspects of outsiders coming into the organisation with risks of fears and jealousies on both sides, that is between the original staff and those introduced as a result of the combination of companies. This also applies to the newcomers, who may sometimes consider themselves superior to the 'old hands'.

8. *Advertising Campaigns.* Employees should not be left to see advertising campaigns only when they appear, but should have advance knowledge. Stills of TV commercials and reproduction of press advertisements or posters should be published in the house journal or displayed on notice boards or special display stands. (This will be similar to advance information released to the sales force, distributors and the

trade press). Where appropriate, there can be video shows of a forthcoming series of TV commericials. Employees are entitled to know how the results of their labour are to be promoted. They may also be invited to express their opinions of the campaign. After all, in many large companies producing FMCGs the employees will also be typical buyers, and their opinions could be representative.

9. *Advisory Information.* Management can help the staff and indirectly help the company if advice is given on new legislation which affects them (e.g. income tax, transport law, state health and pension benefits, savings, life insurance and house purchase schemes). This may be placed on the notice board, distributed direct to individuals if very important, or published in the house journal.

10. *PR Media Coverage.* This may not concern all the staff but managers, salesmen and other interested parties should receive photocopies or office litho reproductions of press cuttings and monitored broadcast material. The mistake should not be made of distributing news releases internally since people may not understand why different versions are published in only some of the journals on the mailing list, or not at all. But distribution of reproductions will make practical use of press cuttings instead of hiding them away in an album in the PR office. Similarly, reprints of PR articles can be distributed. All this can help employees to understand the PR role. Where there is a lot of media coverage it is a good idea to assemble the cuttings as a collection of stapled sheets for, say, weekly or monthly distribution to those who should be informed about PR activity.

11. *Staff Benefits.* Although these will be explained in personal letters or separate publications, internal media may also be used to announce, explain or remind staff of benefit schemes such as pension schemes, home loans, staff discounts, BUPA, HSA and other health schemes, chiropody services and Christmas bonuses.

Under these headings of upwards, sideways and downward communication 24 topics have been suggested, but there could be many more according to the kind of organisation. When analaysed like this, management can see the justification for internal communication systems. They can be recognised as necessities, not luxuries.

PR For The Professions

A number of professional bodies do not permit their members to advertise, and some do not know the difference between advertising and public relations, regarding any contrived publicity as advertising. A feature article could be interpreted as contrived publicity but it is not advertising. Some years ago a doctor was struck off because an article about his private clinic appeared in a foreign magazine. In contrast, lawyers in North America and the Caribbean have defied the rules and advertised their practices. In Britain, the Royal Society of British Architects amended its Code of Practice[15] in 1981 to permit the use of public relations, and an American expert has been allowed to lecture to RIBA members on how to market architectural services. Principle 3, 6.1

permits a member to undertake PR activities and Principle 3, 6.2 of the Code says 'A member may commission an external public relations consultant.' *The Architects Journal* has published advice on press relations.

An American Example

Hill and Knowlton, international PR consultants, refer to public relations for the professions as 'an emerging field.' In the USA, bans on advertising some professions were relaxed, but as Hill and Knowlton state in their *Annual Review*[16], 'Advertising met with little success, since marketing a service - by whatever means - is different from marketing a product. Moreover, the role of the individual in professional firms often overshadows the institutional reputation in the minds of clients, reflecting both the nature of service industries and the entrepreneurial character of the professions.

'In response, we developed techniques and programs that would meet the unique needs and sensitivities of professional firms....we have conducted communications audits to support client practice development efforts and produced marketing materials. We have helped position clients as sources of reliable commentary on developments in law and accounting in cities around the U.S., and, for one client, helped create a journal on new trends in personnel administration and management theory.

'Our Minneapolis office worked with a law firm to develop a highly successful program to recruit graduates from major Northeast law schools. Our offices in Europe and the Far East worked with a management recruiting client on new office openings and on practice development....H & K/Chicago performed two pioneering studies for a law firm, the first designed to assist the clients' recruiting efforts on law school companies and the second, a major strategic planning study, to guide future direction of the firm.'

PR For British Professions

In Britain, the Pharmaceutical Society has produced a manual giving advice to pharmacists on how to conduct PR locally, and has held seminars in London to teach its members PR Practice.

This is an interesting field because many professionals have been, and still are, nervous of being accused of unprofessional behaviour if their names appear in the press, or they appear on television, and this could be misconstrued as advertising or overt publicity seeking. Yet it is very necessary to educate potential clients about their services, and to gain credit for their achievements. Today, many professional institutions and societies make the distinction between advertising and public relations, and permit their members to do more than put their name on a brass plate or on a notice board on a building site. They produce brochures and house journals, issue news releases, publish feature articles, organise seminars, and appear on radio and television as authorities on their subjects. Management consultants, consulting engineers, consulting scientists and others now use PR techniques to create understanding of their services.

Usually, they are protected by codes of practice which both provide self-regulatory controls on their behaviour, and show the world (including critics) that they are committed to professional standards.

This is true of public relations itself. The Institute of Public Relations, the Public Relations Consultants Association, the International Public Relations Association, and national PR institutes and associations throughout the world all have their codes of practice. Such codes stipulate that members must not issue false information, not corrupt the integrity of the media, not mislead by working for a disguised or undisclosed interest, must maintain confidentiality, not represent conflicting interests without consent, not receive payment for the same thing from two sources, not seek payment on the basis of unpredictable forecasts, not indulge in bribery of holders of public office, and not maliciously injure the reputation or practice of other members. This is a very truncated version of the IPR and PRCA codes, but it helps to indicate the high standards of the profession. It also indicates the standards followed by qualified practitioners, and the merit in employing PROs and PR consultants who are members of their respective bodies.

Financial PR

Often coupled with corporate public relations, financial PR has grown in importance in the last twenty years. In the City there are some thirty or more consultancies which specialise in financial PR, while most of the large general consultancies (with offices outside the city) also offer financial services. Hill and Knowlton, from whose *Annual Review* two quotations are taken in this chapter, have both a West End and a City office in London. This area of PR covers the financial affairs of public limited companies and Stock Exchange activities, the financial institutions, investment analysts, shareholders, City editors and the business press. Financial institutions include banks, insurance companies, pension funds, unit trusts, and building societies.

The substance of financial PR consists of interim and annual reports and accounts, private companies going public, new issues and debentures, privatisation share issues, take-over bids and day-to-day news of quoted companies which is of interest to the investment market. Bound up with this will be corporate PR concerning the behaviour of companies. While share prices may be affected by a remarkable variety of external influences, the fall, rise or stability of share prices will be influenced by company performance and stock market confidence. This in turn may depend on how well a company's financial PR is conducted. While it would be foolish to stampede the market by overdoing a company's PR, it does follow that stock market confidence does require adequate and current information about and understanding of a company. Misconceptions can cause mischief as when a company is seen to be engaged in a risky undertaking when in fact other parts of the company are enjoying a very profitable experience.

Why has there been such a boom in financial PR, and not only in the world's money centres such as London, New York and Hong Kong? In many developing countries, such as Nigeria, foreign companies have been indigenised, shares put on the market and stock exchanges opened. In spite of recession in industrialised countries, stock markets have been lively. Although watched by the Monopolies Commission in Britain, take-overs continue to take place. Unit Trusts have become popular. New forms of insurance as forms of investment and savings have become attractive. Nationalised industries and companies like Amersham, BP, Britoil and Cable and Wireless, have been partly or wholly privatised. The banks have introduced new services, and competition rages between them and the building societies. All kinds of plastic money now exist. A whole new intelligence system about the money market has emerged, and it has to be fed with information. Since investment demands confidence it is the very stuff of public relations, which aims to inform and educate in order to create knowledge, understanding, goodwill and reputation.

As an indication of the growth of financial PR in Britain, the city and financial group of the IPR has become a very successful and influential one with 130 members from consultancies and companies.

Take-over bids

When companies are involved in take-over bids, both sides have to inform their shareholders. For the weaker party it may be too late, or almost so, and very likely it is suffering from a lack of PR in the past. The 'victor' has to galvanise last-minute defensive strategies. Advertising becomes the last, and a very expensive, resort. But even a company whose PR has been good may be endangered by business circumstances.

Spillers, for instance, were caught between a strike of bakery workers which forced up labour costs and the demand by supermarkets for cheaper bread. They were squeezed out of the market from both sides, so they shut down their plant bakeries. This had the effect of reducing both turnover and share prices. Dalgety saw the opportunity to take-over. The remarkable final result of this was that Tony Spalding, Spillers PRO, ran such a brilliant campaign to fight off Dalgety, that, when they won, they appointed him as their PRO. Later, Tony Spalding, left Dalgety to produce another brilliant PR campaign for Sea Containers when they launched the Venice-Simplon-Orient-Express.

Walter Raven, City PR consultant, in an interview with Martin Hedges[17] describes his experiences during the attempted takeover of Linfood, and then Linfood's own take-over bid. When Jimmy Gulliver's Argyle Foods bid for Linfood it 'had problems of visibility and profitability....Linfood prepared the classic City defence tactics: it forecast sharply increased profits, increased dividends and revalued the company's assets upwards....Generally speaking, you do anything you were thinking of doing, but hadn't got round to doing. PR's role is to get the City and City journalists to accept the increased profits forecasts as accurate.'

One might ask why hadn't they got round to doing it? Why wasn't the

PR consultant brought in until a desperate situation had arisen? Here we have a case of both crisis PR and financial PR, with management being oblivious to the need for both until it was almost too late, together with the abuse of PR - using it as a fire-fighting exercise.

Quite rightly, Walter Raven goes on to say 'After the frenzy of a take-over bid there is a void. After they've been battered with communications, there's nothing. It is up to the public relations executive to fill this void.'

In the event, Linfood's promise of higher profits was exceeded and as Raven explains 'The Company has to deliver otherwise the share price moves in the wrong direction and the institutional shareholders start asking questions.'

However, in such a situation, all shareholders and everyone interested in the bid have to be fully informed. Small shareholders are bewildered by postal persuasion tactics, and it can be an ugly battle in the City. As Raven says, 'Messages, each with a different emphasis, must be prepared for the small shareholder, the institutional shareholder, investment analyst and the media.'

Hill and Knowlton have a sophisticated system for identifying institutional and significant individual shareholders holding shares through nominees or banks whose shares are held in securities depositories. The consultancy's financial PR services now cover 'mergers, tender offers, proxy fights and hostile take-over attempts[18].' The following description from the brochure of the Hill and Knowlton Proxy Solicitation Group provides a valuable insight into modern PR services:

'We begin each assignment by reviewing data from published sources and records, and information supplied by the client, as well as our own extensive records amassed from years of experience. We are in continuous contact with insurance companies, mutual and pension funds, banks, and money managers for additional information that helps us identify significant beneficial owners.

'The group's computer system compares and cross-references the resulting data to produce reports tailored to a client's needs. Such reports include: lists of large bank depository and nominee holders, analyses of mutual fund holdings and 13-F reporting banks; share range and other analyses of voted proxy cards; lists of foreign holders; and daily or periodic trends in price, volume, and block trades for client, industry, and/or market indices.'

Going Public

When a private company wants funds in order to expand, it 'goes public', offering shares to the public and seeking a Stock Exchange quotation. The success of this operation depends largely on what the market knows about the company, and the faith it has in its prospects. We have witnesed the failure of Britoil and the success of BP in 1982 and 1983, which bears out this need for elementary PR.

But supposing the company has no competitor in the stock market, and it is difficult to place a premium on the share offer, unlike the 1983

BP offer when the underwriters could set both a minimum price and invite a bid price, finishing up with an excellent striking price? This was Rentokil's dilemma, but here was a company built on superb PR over decades, and the new shares were oversubscribed nearly four times at a very good premium.

An example of exceptional confidence occurred when Sainsburys went public. Here was a company which enjoyed the goodwill of thousands of housewives and other customers. There was a unique sale of shares in £5 lots over bank counters.

The Investible Idea

How many managements ask themselves why anyone should buy their shares? This is a challenging aspect of financial PR. It takes us beyond traditional PR which seeks to keep the market informed about a company's activities so that it is fully understood and its investment value appreciated. That may not be enough. It is really no different from asking why customers should buy at one store rather than another, or holiday abroad in this country instead of that. The attractions of, say, oil shares are not just that companies are big and successful. One may pay high dividends even though its share price fluctuates widly, possibly because of world events. Another may have advantages because it receives its oil from a stable part of the world, while yet another may have diversified into other energy fields. it is rather like finding the unique selling proposition of the advertising business.

Most companies will have a number of good reasons why institutions especially should buy their stock, but the market can be confused by too many ideas. It is better to test these 'selling points' so that the PR programme can concentrate on the most powerful one. This process is described in Burson-Marsteller's monograph *The Investible Idea*[19] from which the following is quoted:

> *Developing the Investible Idea*
>
> How does a corporation develop an investible idea - a positioning message that will gain these results?
>
> One example is Houston Natural Gas, a fairly diversified company in the energy business. It has a gas pipeline, searches for gas and oil, has coal and other operations. The search for an investible idea began with speculating about which core messages might be most interesting. One was that the company invests substantially in exploration and has a good discovery record. Another was that it is well diversified and has balance. Another: it has a lot of gas in the ground. A further idea evolved from the concept that the best investments are companies that have high market share in high-growth markets. Texas, with the highest growth, residentially and industrially, of any state, is projected to remain so through the decade, and the biggest part of the company's

business is supplying gas to the state of Texas.

The various messages were mocked up in editorial format with headlines and subheads, and presented for reaction to a series of focus groups and individual investors. The clear winner was the high market share in a high-growth market, and is now the basis of a campaign the company is running. It does not tell everything the investor needs to know about Houston Natural Gas, nor should it; instead it is an investible idea and, as such, seems to be working.

Having established an investible idea, a company should segment its message into three levels. The first of these is the investible idea itself. The second is an enhancement of the idea, and comprises all other points - good management, effective strategic plan, superior research and development - that make the company an attractive investment. The third level is what can be termed 'responsive messages' - responses to questions which can be raised about a corporation.

Financial Fossils

Financial institutions are sometimes accused of fossilization because of their entrenched ideas about reticence and respectability, but a revolution is taking place. We have, for example, seen the more attractive, more shop-like, design of banks and building societies. All kinds of institutions have opened their doors to satisfy public interest.

On the subject of building societies, Michael Megarry, PR manager, Leeds Building Society, has written[20]: 'They now project their image and their products in every way possible. In particular, there has been an expansion of in-house PR departments in those societies which have learned the advantages of an increased public profile. And there has been more community involvement, including full ranges of literature and in-house publicity aids, staff publications, increased media liaison and extra communication with members - the main ingredients of a healthy corporate image.'

Megarry continues: 'The consumer is now better informed than ever before about all kinds of finance - whether it be how his few shares in an obscure company are behaving or what is the best buy from the building societies this week.

'The result is a more financially liberated public, which wants to peek under the covers at the mysterious world of the City. It wants to know about the City's infrastructure, how it operates and what the various component companies and institutions have to offer.'

A good example of how the City itself is educating the public is the PR conducted by the Stock Exchange. The new building was constructed with a special glass-windowed viewing room from which members of the public may look down and observe activity on the floor of the exchange, while a guide explains what is going on. Afterwards, the visiting party is shown a video about the workings of the Stock Exchange.

Parliamentary Liaison and Political Lobbying

The object of parliamentary liaison and political lobbying is not bribery and corruption, although it has been said that only those with sufficient money and muscle can indulge in pressure group activity, and that such representations are denied others less well-off. This is not entirely true as we have seen with those very articulate voluntary groups which have very forcibly expressed their views on subjects such as nuclear disarmament, American missiles, the siting of a third London airport, and proposals for the routing of new motorways. The building of a Carrefour supermarket had to be abandoned when the Minister responded to local opposition.

PR advisers do not seek to entice ministers, MPs or civil servants to do their clients' or employers' bidding. Political PR operates in two ways:

1. *Parliamentary Liaison.* Business interests may be affected by new legislation, debates, enquiries by select committees or Royal Commissions, questions in the House, and other parliamentary activities. It is important, therefore, that the management of companies affected should know when, for instance, a Bill is going through its committee stages. Consultants specialising in Parliamentary liaison are able to advise their clients about Parliamentary procedures. As a result of this knowledge they can engage in lobbying MPs at the right time, make representations to Ministers or civil service chiefs, or offer evidence to select committees and Royal Commissions of enquiry. A description of the services offered by Charles Barker, Watney and Powell is given at the end of this section.

2. *Political Lobbying.* This entails making direct approaches by either individuals or 'lobbies' or 'pressure groups' representing particular interests to Ministers, 'shadow ministers', groups of MPs interested in certain subjects, MPs in general, or senior civil servants in the various ministries and departments. The object of such lobbying is to present the case for the interested party.

Pressure groups seek to influence and produce change, but an interest group may only serve its own interests, and not seek to exert fundamental external changes.

The role of single issue pressure or special interest groups (which have become known as extra-Parliamentary action by extra-Parliamentary groups) was one of the topics discussed at the 1983 IPR Conference on November 3 which had as its theme Politics of Pressure. At this conference, Des Wilson of CLEAR defined pressure groups as 'advocates in the court of public opinion.'

He explained how his pressure group had achieved political response to the issue of lead poisoning, and the case for lead-free petrol. But one reason for the success of the CLEAR campaign was the failure of the opposition pressure groups to present a credible argument. He pointed out that the collapse of public transport in the UK is not only to do with the popularity of the motor-car, but because of the weakness of the public transport lobbies compared with those with vested interests in the motor-car, road haulage and petroleum industries. He went on to say that pressure groups counterbalanced weaknesses in the democratic system, representing minorities. They also combatted other pressure groups, and maintained the momentum and stamina of issues which the media are otherwise inclined to drop.

Is Political PR Ethical?

There is nothing sinister about political PR, although a Labour Government set up a select committee to investigate the relations between MPs and PR practitioners. There was a change of Government, and nothing came of it beyond the voluntary decisions of the IPR and PRCA to each keep a register of members who employ a Member of Parliament, of either House, whether in a consultative or executive capacity. This is written into their codes of conduct.

From time to time the press has tried to read something untoward into the employment of Members of Parliament, forgetting that MPs themselves have to obey the rules of the House and declare their interests. Employment takes two forms: MPs may be legitimately employed as principals, directors or executives of PR consultancies, while MPs may be paid fees or retainers simply to inform clients about Parliamentary procedures as already described. They are not paid to favour any client or cause by asking questions, speaking in debates or in committees, or voting in a certain way.

There is actually a very good case for political PR as part of the democratic process. It enables individual MPs to be better informed on a subject before the House, and it enables Government to have discussions with representative bodies or groups when framing new legislation.

This is, therefore, an area very pertinent to management when business is affected by legislation, controls, taxation and Government policies. But for PR intervention, Government could be unaware of unfair or unwise action which could harm industries and individual firms. There can also be private members bills which could have adverse effects unless these results were made known to MPs before they committed themselves in the voting chamber.

Even private members bills can be costly and dangerous. Some years ago a private member's bill was tabled which resulted in manufacture of a certain poison being made illegal in Britain, in spite of every MP receiving a personal letter from the chairman of the manufacturing company. The poison killed rats. Rats cause bubonic plague. The poison was claimed to kill cruelly. Plague results in cruel deaths to humans. For politicians, British MPs are very sentimental and the Cruel Poisons Act was passed. That could be taken as a failure of PR, but also as an example of the seriousness and difficulty of political PR. Perhaps, from hindsight, the strategy was inadequate and today a specialist Parliamentary liaison consultant would recommend a different tactic.

Parliamentary liaison work also extends to Brussels and Strasburg. For example, Charles Barker, Watney and Powell (with offices in London and Brussels) provide expert advice on briefing and presentation of cases to MPs, ministers, MEPs and the European Commision. They also deal with local government and trade unions.

The following is how Charles Barker, Watney and Powell describe their political services: 'We provide regular advice to clients on parliamentary procedure, timing of legislation and future business in the Commons and the Lords, the policies and influence of factions and pressure groups, and the interests of individual MPs and Peers.

'Our daily information service includes the Order Paper, Hansard, Bills, White and Green Papers, select committee reports and statutory instruments. Our specialists prepare reports on such subjects as the Queen's Speech and the legislative programme, the Budget, and party conference decisions.'

The Modern PR Consultancy

The PR consultancy world has changed rapidly. Only four consultancies had fee incomes in excess of £1m and there was only one which exceeded £2m in 1981, whereas today ten or more are in the £1m bracket and there are some which have topped the £3 million mark. The Public Relations Consultants Association has more than 100 members, and reports that billings rose from £7.8m in 1979 to £22m in 1983.

To some extent this expresses business management's greater use of PR services. In some cases, recession-hit businesses have closed in-house PR departments and turned to consultancies, but the chief reason is that a number of consultancies have diversified their services and so have much more to offer.

They have also been marketing their services more effectively, to mention only the audio tapes offered free by Burson-Marsteller/London, and the excellent VHS video tape *What Price Public Relations?*[21] also offered free by Charles Barker Lyons. In the video Christopher Bosanquet, chief executive, and his team give ten case study accounts of PR exercises they have mounted with measureable results. It gives the lie to the myth of intangible PR. There is a dearth of educational films about PR, but this excellent 20-minute video tape is not merely a business-getter for Charles Barker Lyons, Britain's largest PR consultancy, but a piece of valuable educational material which should be in all schools where PR is taught. The case studies deal with product publicity, staff relations, political PR, financial PR and different methods of evaluating results. A particularly interesting aspect is the emphasis on the quality and not the volume of media coverage.

Some of the large PR consultancies are more like complete service advertising agencies, departmentalised with specialist services, and they are a far cry from the ex-journalist dominated jack-of-all trades outfits which seldom ventured beyond press relations. Now, division of labour is becoming pronounced, but more than that is the expansion into special areas of communication, some of which have already been described in this chapter. It is also interesting that whereas there has been unfortunate antipathy between marketing and public relations (as explained in Chapter One), some PR consultancies have become very marketing orientated. We see this in both fairly new ones such as Roger Haywood and Associates of Norwich, and in fifty-year-old consultancies of American origin like Burson-Marsteller.

Reginald Watts, chairman and chief executive of Burson-Marsteller's British company, has made the point on both his audio-tape *The*

Communication Audit[22], and in an article in *Marketing Week*[23] about looking at PR as an economic tool when further spending on advertising could be less productive. But to quote from his article, Reginald Watts begins by setting the new scene for PR:

'Recent falls in television figures, problems over TV-am, more leisure pursuits (including video) for the high-spending ABs and, above all, soaring costs in the high-reach print media, are encouraging a fresh look at promotional spends....The problem that brand managers face is that it's no good going to the media and traditional research people for an answer to the question: How else can I get my message across?'

The alternative is public relations, seen as an extension of marketing communication. Says Reginald Watts: '...the modern consultancy is becoming more and more like advertising agencies in terms of specialised services carried in-house. It is not unusual now to visit a PR company and find them with services such as design work, market research, specialist placement newsrooms, television training, sponsorship activity, print buying and many others....The drift is clear. Those PR companies interested in winning fast moving product accounts are moving away from the traditional PR disciplines of press editorial, conference organising and big event promotions, towards a real centre-of-the-mix consultancy role.

'The new breed of marketing trained PR consultant starts analysing the advertising, say by asking himself: What is the cost per thousand at the margin on that extra spend this year? Could we reach the target more cheaply through other channels when a certain saturation point in frequency has been passed on TV?'

This is a new concept in PR thinking. It recognises the diminishing returns factor in excessive advertising expenditure. It does not seek to replace advertising, but to be effective when advertising is not. This also invites a bigger spend on PR than is usually the case, and with very tangible rewards as we saw in the reference to the Charles Barker video tape[24]. Moreover, this wider approach to business communications can be more meaningful to management which is marketing-orientated and is looking for results more directly to do with sales and profits. This is not to say that the numerous other forms of PR are not important, but it does bring PR into areas which are more familiar to management, and ones in which cost effectiveness counts.

Sponsorship is a case in point, and the examples have been given in this book and elsewhere[25] of the immense importance placed on sponsorship by leading sponsors such as Cornhill, Cadbury-Schweppes, Canon, Players, Midland Bank, Prudential, Gillette, Coca-Cola, Coral, W.D. & H.O. Wills, the *Sun*, Dunlop and other big spenders on sponsorship.

In 1983, Britain boasted the first publicly quoted public relations consultancy, this being Good Public Relations (named after its chairman Tony Good), which moved up from the Unlisted Securities Market which it entered in 1981, being 'the first company in the marketing services sector to take that step.'[26]

This was the culmination of the growth of Good Public Relations, a consultancy which among varied services had actually increased its handling of new issue business for financial PR clients. Here is an example of the big, modern, multi-service London PR consultancy which demonstrated the growth and versatility of the consultancy business in the midst of recession.

The Good Relations Group plc comprises five companies which specialise in corporate affairs (including a political issues unit), financial PR, design work, and international PR. Tony Good, in his chairman's statement said 'We have found that, in the current recession, organisations have been seeking new, more cost-effective methods of communication to meet increasing competition.'

Who would have believed in the 70s that the poor relation of advertising would be taking over where advertising had ceased to be cost effective? This is doubtless the most revolutionary special action area of modern public relations. The figures are spectacular: Good's turnover rose from £2.59 million in 1981 to £3.40 million in 1982, with a profit increase of 90 percent on a turnover increase of 31 percent.

While it is still true that an advertising campaign may well be a costly failure if the PR has not been done well in advance to educate the market and create a climate in which marketing is possible, the main advance in PR is in the private sector, where PR now takes off where advertising leaves off.

There is nothing new in London-based consultancies having regional offices, and there are of course excellent locally-based consultancies throughout the UK. But an interesting development occured with the creation of Edelman & Associates by Daniel J. Edelman Ltd, a firm of American parentage whose London office enjoys a turnover around £1 million a year. In 1983 the company acquired a number of well-known regional consultancies in Scotland, Northern Ireland, Wales, Birmingham, Manchester, Newcastle, Norwich and elsewhere to form a national network called Edelman and Associates Ltd. The grouping is described as 'national because it is local'[28] and effective because 'national public relations can be intensified locally.' The services offered include community relations, company newspapers, employee communications, local research, promotions and publicity, media monitoring, news gathering, product launches, local radio, regional receptions and exhibitions, and regional television.

Developments in the PR consultancy world are not limited to the big ones, or to international ones of American parentage. There is yet another resemblance to the advertising agency world. Just as the big multi-service consultancies are not unlike the big service advertising agencies of the J. Walter Thompson mould, so there are many medium-size consultancies which are the counterpart of the new breed of creative or *a la carte* advertising agencies. These consultancies specialise in areas of PR such as the travel trade, motor-car industry, the electronics industry, fashion and beauty products, house journal production, exhibitions, sponsorships or financial PR. Many of these specialised consultancies augment the work of in-house PR departments in companies which do not place all or most of the PR with the larger multi-service consultancies of the Charles Barker, Burson-Marsteller, Good Public Relations or Hill & Knowlton type.

REFERENCES

1. Jefkins, Frank, *Public Relations For Marketing Management*, 2nd. Ed, Macmillan, London, 1983
2. Kransdorff, Arnold, Public Hazards And How Some Are Handled. The Management Page, *Financial Times*, London, September 19, 1983
3. Abbott, Howard, *Product Recall Management Guide*, Product Safety, Kingston-upon-Thames, 1983
4. The *Sun*, London, September 22, 1983
5. Slater, Robert, Crisis Public Relations, *IPRA Review*, London, April, 1982
6. Manuel, Vivian, A Crisis Is Coming! *Journal of Communication Management*, International Association of Business Communicators, San Francisco, Vol. 13, No. 2, 1983
7. Slater, Robert, ibid
8. *Product Safety*, Videotape, LEGO Systems A/S, Billund, 1983
9. Manuel, Vivian, ibid
10. *Communication Skills*, Burson-Marsteller Inc, New York, 1982
11. Vines, Steve, *The Guru of Management*, (An interview with Peter Drucker), *Observer*, September 25, 1983, London
12. Sinclair Research Ltd, whole page advertisement, Where wealth accumulates and men decay...., *Observer*, September 25, 1983
13. *Rentokil Roundabout*, video quarterly house magazine, East Grinstead, Autumn, 1982
14. Robins, Mike, *Quality Circles*, Gower Publishing, Aldershot, 1983
15. RIBA Code of Practice, Royal Institute of British Architects, London, 1981
16. *1982 Annual Review*, *Public Relations: The Cutting Edge*, Hill & Knowlton Inc., New York, 1983.
17. Hedges, Martin, PR: An Essential Weapon in Every Takeover Struggle, *Marketing Week*, London, September 16, 1983
18. *1982 Annual Review, Public Relations: The Cutting Edge*, ibid
19. Hughes, Anthony D, *The Investible Idea*, monograph, Burson-Marsteller Financial Relations, New York, 1983
20. Megarry, Michael, Financial Fossils Come Alive, Public Relations Special Report, *Campaign*, September 16, 1983
21. *What Price Public Relations?* VHS videotape, Charles Barker Lyons Ltd, London, 1983
22. Watts, Reginald, *The Communications Audit*, audio-tape, Burson-Marsteller Ltd, London, 1982
23. Watts, Reginald, Checking Out New Methods of Putting the Message Across, *Marketing Week*, London, September 16, 1983
24. *What Price Public Relations*, ibid
25. Jefkins, Frank, *Public Relations Made Simple*, Heinemann, London, 1982
26. Jones, Simon, Good Makes its Move Upwards, City Analysis, *Marketing Week*, September 9, 1983.
27. Good, Anthony, *Report & Accounts 1982*. Good Relations Group PLC, London
28. *National Public Relations*, Edelman and Associates, London, October, 1983.

9.

ASSESSMENT OF RESULTS

The best way to assess results is to begin with objectives, as demonstrated in Chapter Three on tangible public relations. Evaluation may be by a scientific method, using research techniques, or by observation and experience. Thus we have both quantitative and qualitative methods of assessment. When marketing research methods have been applied to the appreciation of the situation the same methods can be repeated at intervals, but certainly at the conclusion of the PR programme. Shifts of opinion, improvements in awareness or more accurate perception of the image can be measured. Two main methods may be used, the opinion poll and the image study.

Opinion Poll

Made famous by Gallup, the opinion poll concentrates on questions to which Yes, No, Don't Know answers are given, these being computed to show the percentage of people who hold negative or positive opinions, or express no particular opinions. Applied to a public relations enquiry, it is possible to discover attitudes to a company, and in subsequent surveys to test how these attitudes have altered as a result of PR activities. Other types of questions can be included in questionnaires to ascertain, for instance, what percentage of the sample have heard of the organisation or know what it does. Comparisons can be made with knowledge about rival organisations. This method was used before and after Cornhill Insurance sponsored test cricket. It was found that the company scored a very low figure in comparison with other leading British insurance companies, but after the first year of sponsorship the number of people who were aware of Cornhill was increased nine times. During the Tests the number of radio and TV mentions were monitored, and press coverage was assessed.

Image Study

An image study is conducted rather differently. The sponsor of the survey is compared with a number of rival companies, the respondents being unaware of the identity of the sponsor. They are asked how they would rate each company on a number of issues such as price, delivery, service, research or whatever is characteristic of the companies. These ratings are shown graphically so that the comparisons are demonstrated visibly. The sponsor is thus able to see how his customers see him in comparison with his rivals, sometimes better sometimes worse. The results can be enlightening, and will show perhaps how the external current image of the company differs from the internal mirror image. For instance, the sponsor may believe that he is a leader on quality, delivery, research or after-sales service only to find that customers rate him as inferior to all or some of his rivals. He will also learn the strengths and weaknesses of his rivals as perceived by his customers. Later, at the close of a PR programme, a further survey will show to what extent his efforts to improve weak areas have been made sufficiently well-known and understood for the graphs to respond in his favour.

Communication Audit

These may be studies of either internal or external communications, or a blend of both and different consultancies adopt slightly different techniques. They may use structured questionnaires and produce quantitative reports, or depth interviews and group discussions to produce qualitative findings. A general communication audit, like that of Burson-Marsteller, will inform management of the attitudes held by people inside and outside the organisation.

On the other hand, where there is a serious breakdown or lack of communications in a large company, a survey of communications problems from top to bottom of the company can be conducted, and this sort of study may take from two to six months according to the size of the company and the varieties of employee groups. If the recommendations were adopted, it would be sensible to carry out a later internal communications audit to test the extent of change and improvement.

Measuring Media Coverage

How does one measure editorial and programme coverage in the press and on radio and television? A yardstick which used to be applied, and still is by Americans, is to multiply the space or time by its advertisement rate-card cost. But it does not take much thought to realise that this is a false and misleading evaluation. Editorial space and news or programme time is priceless. Moreover, such space or airtime in such quantities on those days, in or on that media would never be contemplated in an advertising schedule. A sponsored event might occupy one hour or more of airtime but it would be prohibitive to buy such a volume of time for advertising purposes. There is therefore no comparison. Again, the PR message differs from advertising and is in no way a form of advertising. Let us therefore consider some more realistic ways of appraising media coverage.

Volume Assessments

There are three ways of making volume assessments of media coverage. First, the number of column inches or centimetres, or minutes of radio or TV airtime, can be totalled. Second, the number of mentions on radio or TV can be counted, as with a sponsorship when commentators refer to, say, the Cornhill Test. Third, the opportunities to see (OTS) can be measured in terms of readership or audience figures derived from JICNARS[1], JICRAR[2] or BARB[3] surveys of the press, radio and TV respectively.

Quality Assessments

Much more realistic still are studies of the quality of the coverage. In which publications or programmes was the story used? Were they influential or unimportant? A small report in the *Financial Times* might be more significant than a column in the *News of the World*, and vice versa according to the nature of the story. A report on *News At Ten* might be more valuable than one on Capital Radio. One women's magazine or trade magazine may be more important to the company than another. Publications can be given ratings, which could be different for different companies, products or services. The following is an example of a rating chart in which the smaller circulation 'heavies' or serious newspapers are more valuable to the sponsor of the stories.

Publication	Rating	Story 1	Story 2	Story 3
The Times	10	X	X	X
Financial Times	10		X	X
Daily Telegraph	8	X	X	X
The Guardian	7			
Daily Express	6			X
Daily Mail	5	X		
Daily Mirror	2		X	
The Sun	2	X		
	Score	25	30	34

Fig. 3 Press Coverage Ratings Chart

This sort of value judgement or cost benefit can be taken further if other factors such as the value of the page where the story appeared, the day of appearance, the tone of the report, whether a picture was used and so on are added to the volume, the opportunities to see and the rating value. All this information can be put into a computer to produce a figure representing all the values. After a time, an average score can be taken as standard against which future scores can be compared.

Quality may also consist of coverage by media which previously took no interest, perhaps deliberately because of hostility or prejudice, or because editors had not appreciated that the subject was of interest and value to their readers or audiences. There could also be changes in editorial attitudes which could now be more sympathetic. There could also be greater accuracy in reports and comments now that the subject was better understood by journalists and broadcasters. These could be very tangible results. They are more sensible and informative than an assessment that so much space or airtime would have cost so much had it been bought as advertising media. That sort of assessment says nothing for the PR value.

Yet another way of reckoning the value of media coverage could be the number of enquiries received. Some journals, mainly trade and technical ones, operate a reader service and invite enquiries which are then forwarded to the companies concerned. This has an additional value: the source of enquiries will reveal whether the journal is read by the people with whom the company wishes to communicate, and whether further PR material should or should not be sent to it.

Photography can be an expensive item in the PR budget, and the indiscriminate issue of pictures with news releases can be wasteful. A check on the use of pictures supplied could reveal those journals which never or seldom print the company's pictures. As a result of this test, pictures could in future be restricted to those journals which use them regularly, or a postscript could be added to the news release stating pictures were available. Reproductions of available pictures can also be included in or with the news release, saving not only the cost of prints but captioning time, hard-backed envelopes and extra postage. A typical example of picture wastage is with appointment stories which seldom gain more than a few lines of editorial.

Evaluation of Observation or Experience

Not every result will require research, and statistical evidence. Some of the more qualitative results can be seen to happen as when the whole atmosphere of staff relations and the stability of staff is self-evident. The calibre and appropriateness of job applicants can also be observed.

Improvements in community relations can be experienced in dealings with local people and organisations, including public services and the local authority. Even invitations to participate in local events can indicate new respect for the company. It can matter how parents,teachers, clergymen, policemen and taxi-cab drivers speak about the company. Residents may speak with pride that they come from the town where the company is located. A lot of healthy PR can be derived from having ambassadors in the community. A good neighbour policy works both ways.

The corporate image reflects how a company is seen to behave. Sponsorships, the public activities of management personalities, the quality of research, the industrial relations record, trading results, and social responsibility on environmental issues all contribute to the corporate image. Research can assess this, but goodwill and reputation can also be judged by how the company is regarded at large. One seldom if ever hears criticism of Marks and Spencer who in recent years have been complimented by both the Prime Minister and Prince Charles. Such accolades and esteem are not enjoyed by companies with poor corporate images. These images have to be earned, but PR can make known why they are deserved, and this can be observed in relations with all the company's publics.

A fall in complaints or an increase in recommendations can be observed, and they can result from a campaign of market education. Improved dealer relations can be seen not only in higher sales and bigger orders, but in attitudes towards the company and towards sales representatives during their calls, in prompt payment of accounts, greater willingness to use displays or to participate in sales promotion schemes. These could be the results of dealer education programmes comprised of dealer magazines, conferences, works visits, videos of forthcoming TV commercials, invitations to exhibitions, and trade press relations.

The results of financial and shareholder relations can be seen in the interest taken by City editors, the readiness of the financial press to recommend a company's shares, and in the actual performance of share prices. There are shares that do not move many points in either direction in spite of world events which cause violent fluctuations in other share prices. These are usually shares which are bought by the institutions even when the market is not buoyant. They are sometimes the ones which go on climbing steadily until the company finds it expedient to make scrip issues such as two for one. Good shareholder relations - which may be assisted by sending shareholders the house journal instead of communicating with them merely to announce interim and annual results - can result in shares being held on to, and this loyal base can be valuable should there be a take-over bid. Such stability can occur when a company does not pay very high dividends, but re-invests and keeps the market aware of its growth intentions and potential. This makes good news, shows confidence, maintains or increases share prices, and retains shareholders.

In Chapter Three some 40 tangible objectives were cited. These were all aims which could be achieved by public relations. A number of methods and examples have been set out in this chapter, but it all depends what objectives have been set in the proposed programme. Most results will be quite simply the achievement of the precise objectives on which the plan was based. The reason for planning a PR programme is to achieve desired objectives, and there should be no doubt or mystery about the success or otherwise of the plan. The overall aim is management success in whatever it sets out to do.

REFERENCES

1. Joint Industry Committee for National Readership Surveys, London
2. Joint Industry Committee for Radio Audience Research, London
3. Broadcasters' Audience Research Board, London.

10.

PR PROFESSIONALISM

Public relations is a profession in the sense that it is an advisory service, its practitioners can obtain professional qualifications, and it has a professional institute whose members are required to uphold a code of conduct. In Britain there is the Institute of Public Relations and in the USA the Public Relations Society of America, both founded in 1948. There are similar bodies in most countries. There are also specialised bodies, and also international associations. In addition, there are independent vocational examining bodies such as the Communications, Advertising and Marketing Educational Foundation and the London Chamber of Commerce and Industry.

In appointing either in-house PR practitioners or an outside PR consultancy, management should be aware of the memberships and qualifications to be expected of them. Distinguishing letters such as MIPR do represent training, experience and standards. Unfortunately anyone can call himself a PRO or a PR consultant: the only reliable yardstick which can be applied is his appropriate membership. For instance, full membership of the IPR does mean a minimum of five years comprehensive experience. A person cannot just join, but has to go through a screening process by the Membership Committee before being elected by Council. Applications may be held up until adequate information is supplied, applicants with less than the required experience are offered lower grades of membership, and some are rejected altogether. Advertising and journalism are not counted as PR experience. Fellowships are rare, and are based on detailed citations showing the sponsored persons's outstanding contribution to public relations, and usually he must have been in membership for 10 years. Even then, not every proposal for Fellowship is accepted by Council.

Institute of Public Relations

Although a national professional body, the IPR does have overseas members in some 50 countries, and it is the senior PR organisation in Britain and the largest PR organisation in Europe. It has more than 2,500 individual members in categories of Honorary Fellow, Honorary Member, Fellow, Member, Associate and student.

The chief objectives of the Institute are:

(a) To promote the development, recognition and understanding of public relations.

(b) To establish and prescribe standards of professional and ethical conduct and to ensure the observance of such standards.

(c) To encourage the attainment of professional academic qualifications.

(d) To provide via meetings, conferences, seminars, printed material, information discussion and comment on all aspects of the practice of public relations.

(e) To maintain two-way contact between the public relations profession in the UK and public relations practitioners throughout the world.

Council consists of members elected for three years, after which they must stand down for a year before seeking re-election. There are also elected area group representatives. The president and honorary treasurer are elected by the members annually. There is a Board of Management and Public Relations, Professional Practices, Membership, Membership Development, Education, Member Services and International Relations committees. Area Groups, Vocational or Special Interest Groups extend the activities of the Institute.

It is a condition of membership that the Code of Professional Conduct is upheld. The Institute publishes a Register of Members. Its journal *Public Relations*[1] is one of the best PR Journals in the world, and it has twice won a BAIE Award of Excellence. A monthly Newsletter is also published. An annual conference is held, and also lunch-time meetings and a number of functions such as the President's Reception and the Fellows Dinner.

The Institute is a constituent member of the Communication, Advertising and Marketing Education Foundation (CAM) which in 1969 combined the IPR examinations with those of the Advertising Association and the Institute of Practitioners in Advertising. An IPR representative serves on the CAM Board of Governors and Education Committee.

Public Relations Consultants Association

Founded in 1969, the PRCA has corporate members, these being about 100 of the leading PR consultancies in the UK with a few overseas members. They represent the bulk of consultancy business, and in the 80s they have enjoyed a growth rate exceeding 20 per cent per annum.

The chief objectives of the Association are:

(a) The improved awareness and status of public relations consultants and the PRCA.

(b) Improving management capability in member consultancies.

(c) Extending the constituency from which consultancies draw their clients.

(d) Raising professional standards of practice at all levels.

The Association is governed by an elected Board of Management, and has a elected chairman, vice-chairman, and honorary treasurer.

There are Professional Practices and Consultancy Management committees, and the PRCA is represented on the CAM Board of Governors.

With some variations to suit consultancy practice, the Association's Code of Professional Practice resembles the IPR code. In conjunction with the *Financial Times*, it publishes the *Public Relations Yearbook*[2]. Other publications include a monthly Newsletter, guidance papers, case studies and from time to time the PRCA conducts useful research.

The PRCA is a source of advice when management is seeking to appoint a PR consultant.

Another source is the *Hollis Press and Public Relations Annual*[3]. This comprehensive annual lists the majority of PR consultancies in the UK (including non-members of the PRCA), together with client lists in many cases, plus the addresses of PR Institutes and PR consultancies throughout the world.

British Association of Industrial Editors

This is a very active body founded in 1949 and representing more than 1000 commercial and industrial house journal editors reponsible for some two thousand printed sponsored or private journals plus audio-visual communications such as video magazines.

The principal pbjectives are the BAIE are:

(a) To develop the skills of members.

(b) To promote a regular exchange of ideas and experience between members on communication techniques.

(c) To provide education in all aspects of industrial editing and encourage other educational bodies to do so.

(d) To convince organisations that effective communication promotes good relationships and business efficiency.

(e) To improve standards of organisational communications and provide an expert consultancy service for members and managements.

(f) To co-operate with other organisations concerned in the work of organisational communications.

Publications include the monthly *BAIE News*, the bi-annual *BAIE Magazine*, the quarterly *Communication Europe*, a directory of members, and the excellent handbook *BAIE Editors Handbook*[4] which contains practical advice on editing. Among its activities are training seminars, an annual convention, and BAIE's well-known yearly house journal competition which made two Awards of Excellence to the IPR quarterly, *Public Relations*. In recent years election to full membership has been made dependent on either examination or proof of suitability, applicants being first admitted as Associates. Fellows are elected who are considered to be of the highest professional standing, have been in membership for five years, and have had at least ten years experience in the communications field. There are day-release and correspondence courses for the Association's two-part examination.

International Public Relations Association

This para-national body founded in 1949 comprises senior PR practitioners with international interests, and has more than 750 individual members in some 62 countries. Members have to have a minimum of five years experience.

The Association has an International Code of Ethics (the Code of Athens) which is different from the IPR and PRCA codes, being based on the United Nations Declaration of Human Rights.

A series of impressive World Congresses, with attendances by some 1500 delegates have been held every three years since 1958. They were held in London (1979), Bombay (1982) and Amsterdam (1985). Each year, the IPRA Council meets in a different country, e.g. Egypt (1983) and Canada (1984).

The *IPRA Newsletter* is published every two months while the quarterly *IPRA Review*[5] is an authoritative learned journal containing papers and case studies by eminent international PR practitioners. The *Review*, edited by Sam Black, covers all aspects of public relations theory and practice; interprets public relations in its widest sense as incorporating the related fields of public affairs, public relations, communication and human behaviour; and aims to promote and maintain the highest possible standards of ethics, practice and performance in the profession.

There is also a Register of Members with portraits of members, and Awards include a Gold Paper Award for a study of a relevant subject, and an annual President's Award. The Association has taken a leading role in proposing standards for professional education and qualifications at university level, one of the Gold Papers being devoted to this topic.

Management interested in developing understanding of public relations would benefit from subscribing to the two journals. *Public Relations* (IPR) and the *IPRA Review*, both of which are published by Longman.

International Association of Business Comunicators

With a growing UK chapter, the IABC does not conflict with the other bodies described so far because it is an international body concentrating mainly on internal or organisational communications. It has numerous chapters in Canada and the USA, one in the UK and members in more than 45 countries. The head office is in San Francisco, but it maintains a secretariat in Britain.

The IABC is noteworthy for the excellence of its conferences, seminars, publications and member services. A Gold Quill award is made rather like the BAIE annual competition. Ideas files are available. The membership directory is an impressive volume since there are more than 10,000 members, making it the largest communications organisation in the world. Members range over house journal editors, consultants and academics. The IABC publishes the monthly *IABC News*, the quarterly *Communications World* and a newsletter for overseas members.

Ordinary membership is by application, but Accredited Membership is granted to those who submit a portfolio of their work and experience, pass an intensive four-hour written examination, and submit a verbal solution to a communications problem which is presented to them during the examination, this being taped for the examiners. Accredited members use the letters ABC.

Communication, Advertising and Marketing Education Foundation

Founded in 1969, CAM came about as the independent examining body for the professional examinations of the Advertising Association and the Institute of Practitioners in Advertising, and was joined by the Institute of Public Relations which had been contemplating its own examinations to diploma level. Affiliated to CAM are 23 professional institutes and associations representing the British communications industry. The CAM Diploma is recognised world-wide, and there are CAM students in some 40 countries.

The examinations consist of the Certificate in Communications Studies, six subjects having to be passed, this usually taking two years. When the Certificate has been gained, candidates may proceed to the final Diploma (Dip CAM), taking three subjects, or five for Honours.

For the Certificate, six subjects must be passed from the following seven: Marketing, Advertising, Public Relations, Media, Research and Behavioural Studies, Communication Practice, or Business and Economic Environment. For the Diploma, students may specialise in the subjects of greatest use in their future careers, and may be chosen from: International Advertising and Marketing, Consumer Advertising and Marketing, Industrial Advertising and Marketing, Advanced Media Studies, Management Resources, Public Relations for Commercial Organisations, Public Relations for Non-Commercial Organisations, Public Relations Strategy, Marketing Strategy or Market Research. For the CAM Diploma (PR) candidates take the three public relations subjects.

Throughout the communications business, the CAM Diploma has become the recognised professional qualification, and it is of near degree standard. Graduates with accepted experience may join the CAM Society and use the letters MCAM.

Details are given in the *Regulations and Syllabuses* published in June[6].

London Chamber of Commerce and Industry

The LCCI is Britain's oldest business studies examining body, and celebrated its centenary in 1984. The group Diploma in Public Relations is awarded for passes in Public Relations plus two subjects selected from Advertising, Marketing, and Selling and Sales Management, all three being taken in the same Spring or Autumn examinations.

The examinations have become increasingly popular in the UK, but the LCCI has long been established as an international examining body with centres in about 80 countries. While the CAM exams are much sought after by overseas students who cherish a British qualification, the CAM papers tend to be difficult for them because the syllabuses and questions are UK-orientated. This is not the case with the LCCI examinations in which questions are set which invite answers based on lcoal knowledge, experience and conditions. Passes are awarded at pass, credit and distinction levels. Credits or Distinctions in Public Relations, Advertising and Marketing qualify for exemption from the same subjects in the CAM Certificate examinations. It is therefore possible for a diligent student to gain both the LCCI Diploma in Public Relations and half the CAM Certificate in Communication Studies at the same time.

Details are given in the *Regulations, Syllabuses and Timetables*[7] published in June.

Addresses

The addresses of the IPR, IPRA, PRCA, BAIE, IABC, CAM and LCCI are given in the Appendices. However, organisations do change their addresses from time to time, and the latest information will be found in the *Hollis Press and Public Relations Annual*[8], a directory which senior management will find useful to have in their offices. Certainly, *Hollis* is a valuable work of reference for any company library.

REFERENCES

1. *Public Relations*, Longman Group Ltd, Harlow, quarterly.
2. *Public Relations Yearbook*, Financial Times Business Publishing, London.
3. *Hollis Press and Public Relations* Annual, Hollis Directories, Sunbury-on-Thames.
4. *BAIE Editor's Handbook*, British Association of Industrial Editors, Tunbridge Wells, 1982.
5. *IPRA Review*, Longman Group Ltd, Harlow, quarterly.
6. *Regulations and Syllabuses*, CAM Education Foundation, London, June.
7. *Regulations, Syllabuses and Timetables*, London Chamber of Commerce and Industry, Examinations Board, Sidcup, June.
8. *Hollis Press and Public Relations Annual*, ibid.

11.

SETTING UP A PR DEPARTMENT

Some of the differences between public relations and advertising have been explained in this book. Among them are that public relations aims to inform, educate and create understanding, whereas advertising seeks to persuade and sell; public relations needs to be unbiased if it is to be credible, but advertising is inevitably biased if it is to succeed; public relations has to deal with unfavourable as well as favourable situations, quite unlike advertising which promotes selling points; the biggest single cost in public relations is time, but in advertising it is the cost of space and airtime plus production. Another major difference is that while most advertising personnel are engaged in advertising agencies, the majority of PR practitioners are employed in-house.

Although there have been changes in recent years, and as described in Chapter Eight several of the larger consultancies are beginning to resemble complete service advertising agencies with their specialised departments and staff, many PR practitioners work in commercial firms. But PR is not limited to the private or commercial sector, and it is conducted by numerous other organisations which engage in little or no advertising. Government departments, local authorities, health authorities, water services, educational establishments, the police, fire brigade, ambulance service, the Armed Forces, political parties, trade unions, trade associations, professional institutes, charities and other voluntary bodies all employ PROs. Together, these PROs, far exceed those engaged in the business or industrial world. This is because PR applies to any organisation, commercial or non-commercial. These remarks may help management to appreciate yet again that PR is very different from advertising.

So, while advertising will be found in the marketing department this is not the best place to position public relations. In practice, this may not always be so, either because the marketing side of the business has been first to adopt in-house PR services, or because management has not fully understood the more comprehensive role of PR.

Management Must Know What It Wants

Public relations will serve a company best when management knows what it wants from PR. The initiative must come from the top. The correct positioning of the PRO and the PR department will enable management to enjoy the greatest possible value from PR. It is significant that in our most successful companies, the PRO reports directly to the CEO, and is often a board member. He is not tucked away, obscurely, in the marketing department. Nor is he merely a press officer.

Obviously, much depends on the type of company and its communication needs, and also whether it is a FMCG company or one with more specialised, technical or industrial interests. The former may be a big spender on advertising, while the latter may depend more on market education. But for PR to service the entire organisation, and not just marketing, it is necessary for PR to be positioned independently and close to management. This is not to say that PR should not also be marketing-orientated, and in an industrial company which is a modest advertiser the PRO may well be responsible for advertising too.

The following chart, from another book[1] by the author, demonstrates the ideal positioning of the PRO, PR Manager, Communications Manager, or whatever he may be called:

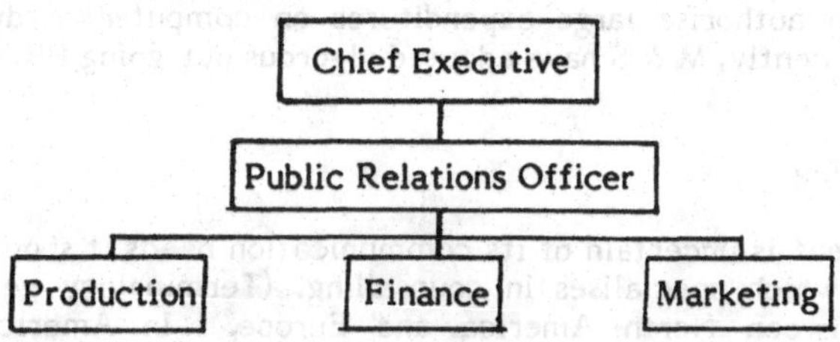

Fig. 4 Positioning of PR in Organisational Structure.

This is an oversimplified chart but it does demonstrate the place of the PRO in relation to the three main functions of most businesses, production, finance and marketing. They in turn embrace corporate affairs, staff relations, financial relations, dealer and customer relations and perhaps export and/or international relations. Political PR, crisis PR and PR to do with environmental and other pressure groups problems will come under corporate PR. In some large organisations, corporate PR may be the responsibility of a public affairs officer. Every company will develop the kind of communications system it requires, and it is arguable whether there should be separate public affairs and public relations functions. To some extent it depends on the size and nature of the business. Sometimes the term public affairs is used merely out of dislike for public relations, and at other times there is a clear division of responsibilities. Whatever the labels, it all amounts to public relations as indicated by the names and memberships of our institutes and associations, and the titles of our journals. So, for simplicity in this book we will stick to public relations as the all-embracing term.

However this specialism is described by Good Relations (Corporate Affairs) Ltd[2] as getting to 'know and understand better what is going on in politics and society generally in a way that is directly relevant to your business. You also need to be able to do something about it if necessary.'

In deciding to set up a public relations department management must know what it wants. This does imply in the first instance an understanding of PR itself, and an ability to buy and use PR services. What are management's communication problems and needs? Does it know what they are?

When Rentokil first set up a PR department in 1959 it did so because almost anybody and any organisation could be a customer, advertising to such a vast, assorted and often specialist market was prohibitive in cost and in many cases ineffective, and market education was a primary need. Unless the market understood how pests lived and what they did it was impossible to sell pest control products and services.

In the case of Marks and Spencer, who rarely advertise, PR has for decades been inherent in board room philosophy, and has been evidenced in merchandise purchasing, shop design, shop hygiene, staff and customer relations. Market education has been a primary form of communication in IBM ever since its inception, and that has included educating those who have to authorise large expenditures on computer hardware and software. Recently, M & S have adopted vigorous out-going PR.

PR Counselling

If management is uncertain of its communication needs it should engage a PR firm which specialises in counselling. (Terminology gets rather strained between North America and Europe. In America, a PR consultant is called a PR counsellor, but in Britain the distinction is usually made that a counsellor advises a client whereas a consultant conducts PR on a client's behalf. A British PR counsellor could thus advise on the setting up of an in-house PR department, and a consultancy may include both advisory and creative services).

Writing A Job Specification

To be really precise, a job specification should be prepared setting out the range of duties which the PRO should undertake for the company. This will reveal three things:

(a) The volume of work that has to be done, and hence the number of staff required.

(b) The extent of specialisation, and so the kinds of staff required.

(c) The qualifications and experience required of the PRO.

The volume of work may be proposed by the PR counsellor who, again, may have recommended research to identify the company's communication needs. It is rarely wise for management to appoint a PRO for minor, isolated, or hastily conceived reasons. Too often, PROs are appointed to protect management from aggresive media, because rival firms use PR, or simply for product publicity. These are trivial reasons, and do not get to the heart of the matter as was shown in Chapter Three on objectives and tangible PR. The volume of work, the workload, should be measured against the effort needed to achieve set objectives.

It should be remembered that whereas in advertising an advertising agency will be appointed because special skills such as creativity and media buying are required, and as these are seldom required every day and the client can enjoy sharing the services of an agency team, this is not so in public relations. Successful PR, and justification for setting up an internal PR department, lies in the PRO knowing the company inside out and being able to work with everybody in it. Thus he is able to service every department, and be able to obtain information quickly when he needs it. While a consultancy has certain other advantages, it can suffer from remoteness and lack of intimacy with the internal workings of an organisation. Public relations is an on-going activity which justifies employment of an in-house PR department.

It is seldom sufficient to make PR a part-time occupation of, say, the advertising manager if the company engages in a lot of advertising. Nor is it usually a good idea to permit an advertising agency to handle PR (unless it has an independent subsidiary company), as advertising agencies rarely understand PR.

The extent of specialisation will depend on whether the PR department requires a house journal editor, press officer, photographer or possibly, nowadays a film and/or video producer. (The latter, however, can be a separate undertaking - linked to PR - which will also produce safety, induction and training programmes). According to the type of business, so specialists may be required to deal with the organisation of seminars, conferences, talks, radio and television appearances, publications of all sorts, private exhibitions, a travelling cinema and so on.

But a full-scale PR department may not be necessary. Many a company has no more than a PRO, an assistant and one or two secretaries. These secretaries are also of the PA type who can assist with PR activities such as press receptions. In this case, the PRO will be an all-rounder, capable of performing a variety of PR tasks. His work may be augmented from time to time by engaging the *ad hoc* or specialist services of freelance writers, video producers, exhibition designers, house journal producers or consultancies specialising in, say, sponsorship, financial PR or Parliamentary liaison.

The third consideration, the qualifications and experience of the PRO, is all important. It is not sufficient to give sideways promotion to an existing executive, nor to give PR responsibility to someone who is being groomed for top management. Nor, as already mentioned, should PR be part of the work of the advertising manager, sales promotion manager, personnel manager or even the marketing manager. This happens - and in some very big companies! - but it hardly recognises the need for particular skills, however familiar the person may be with the company. One would not expect a surgeon to be a chemist, or an architect to be a builder.

To take charge of a company's public relations in all its manifestations, three requirements are advisable:

(a) Membership of the Institute of Public Relations, which indicates that his or her experience has been recognised, and ideally possession of the DipCAM which indicates professional training.

(b) Practical experience in the areas of PR relevant to the company, and its PR objectives.

(c) Possibly some knowledge of the particular industry.

The third requirement may or may not be essential since the principles of PR are applicable to any subject. One of the leading PROs mentioned in this book has worked in the motor-car, foods and travel industries, and another has been engaged in chemicals, department stores and electronics. A well-known bank PRO was once in the fertiliser business.

Should the PRO be a man or a woman? Women are extremely successful in PR, not because they have pretty faces but because they are naturally meticulous over detail. Public relations is mostly hard work.

In making an appointment five basic attributes should be looked for:

(a) Ability to communicate, whether it be through the written or spoken word, or through the media of photography, films and video.

(b) Ability to organise, which means painstaking attention to detail.

(c) Ability to get on with people, that is, like and understand all sorts of people, not flatter them.

(d) Have integrity so that he or she enjoys the confidence of people inside and outside the organisation.

(e) Have imagination, which is necessary in all creative work and in planning events.

Should he or she be a journalist? Not necessarily. A very experienced journalist could be valuable because, apart from writing ability and knowledge of the press, he could be broadly experienced in the ways of the world and business. But not all PR is concerned with press relations, and today PROs are recruited from many fields. A journalist may know little about radio or TV, printing, photography, exhibitions or conference organising, nor, for that matter, about business organisation or marketing. A graduate with business experience may well prove to be better material for PR. As yet, there is little preparation for direct entry to a PR career, as there is in most other professions, and PR is more often a second or third career. For this reason, PR management calls for maturity or at least five years practical experience. Ability to direct staff, plan and budget campaigns, and be accountable in both finances and results, is important for it is, after all, a management job. It is not a job for the chairman's nephew.

Management and Existing PR Departments

In companies which already have a PR department, a long-standing problem is getting management to understand the value and importance of what it is doing, and how they can co-operate and contribute. This may be because the PR department is wrongly positioned in the first place, especially if it is within marketing. Again, sometimes the work of the PRO is frustrated because management keeps him at arms length and relegates him to a low status position. This may be because the PRO has failed to earn higher status, or because too junior a person was appointed, perhaps for the wrong purpose. A common cry heard on many PR seminars is 'If only management could attend this course!'

An interesting view of credibility was expressed by Don Stephenson[3], director of corporate communications for Dow Chemical Canada, who wrote that 'To improve the climate *for* your company, it is first necessary to change the climate *in* your company.'

This poses an interesting new look at the role of the in-house PRO. It has long been held that a bad company image cannot be polished (as the advertising and media pundits pretend), and that a good image may well depend on the PRO insisting that wrong things be put right before a good image can be deserved. But Stephenson stresses that a management environment must be created to 'promote socially responsible corporate performance.' A company is judged by its behaviour, and that includes the behaviour of its people, particularly when they act as spokesmen.

To create this management environment, Stephenson was able to develop the philosophy laid down in the 70s by the then chairman Carl Gerstacker who had postulated that the profit motive be linked with the idea of corporate social responsibility. So, Stephenson produced a booklet called *Dow's Secret Weapons* which contained quotations from speeches made by Dow executives and directors, and some authorities like Robert Townsend and Peter Drucker. This was circulated to senior company personnel, and later to others who requested copies. The campaign to 'raise managers' awareness of the sensitivities and perceptions of the world *outside* the plant gate' continued with 'a television and radio training course for top executives, managers in key positions and certain of our technical experts.'

The programme not only won the CEO's respect for the company's PR function, but gained the co-operation of managers in conducting external PR for the company. 'Most important', says Stephenson, 'the training experience showed a lot of our people that a "no comment", an evasive answer, or a slow response clearly implies guilt. It brought home to them dramatically the shortsightedness of the low profile strategy.'

Stephenson's article concluded with this paragraph:

> 'Credibility is an essential part of our company's growth strategy. Our own credibility is the foundation for our acceptance within Dow. And it's based on gaining management's respect for our intelligence, for our thorough knowledge of communications and the media, our courage in standing up for our professional judgement, for our integrity, and for our ability to serve the company at the same time that we serve the public interest.'

The Dow Canada programme emphasises three aspects of in-house PR:

(a) The PR department cannot operate effectively unless it is understood, respected and supported by management throughout the company.

(b) The PRO should integrate PR inside the company for he is only the specialist or catalyst, and many company personnel will be involved in projecting the company image. There is always the danger of individuals creating a confusing multiple image.

(c) He cannot do his job if other people are undermining the credibility of the company, and that can include the CEO if he is a poor communicator.

In a sense, while the CEO is the captain of the ship, the PRO is the helmsman.

All this implies that when setting up an in-house PR department, and appointing its manager or director, the CEO should choose someone who has the experience, maturity and personality to be able to co-ordinate all the communication strengths in a company, and short-circuit all its weaknesses. This does not stop at company leaders. The telephonist, gate-keeper, van-driver, order clerk, accounts clerk and others who have contact with customers are all part of a company's communication network. Each and every one of them can make or mar a company's reputation. If a ship had only a captain and helmsman on board it would get nowhere. Everyone in a company can be part of its PR team, provided the CEO appreciates this and the PRO possesses the status to inspire it. Consequently a PRO should be appointed and positioned so that he is worthy of this status.

REFERENCES

1. Jefkins, Frank, *Public Relations Made Simple*, Heinemann, London, 1982.
2. *Public Affairs - Managing the Politics of Change*, Good Relations (Corporate Affairs) Ltd, London.
3. Stephenson, Donald R, Internal PR Efforts Further Corporate Responsibility: A Report from Dow Canada, *Public Relations Quarterly*, New York, Summer, 1983.

APPENDIX 1:

BIBLIOGRAPHY

Annual Publications

Benn's Press Directory, Benn Publications Ltd., Tunbridge Wells, Kent.
Contact, (Directory of news contacts), Simon Books Directories, Folkestone, Kent.
Hollis Press and Public Relations Annual, Hollis Directories, Sunbury-on-Thames, Middlesex.
Public Relations Yearbook, Financial Times Business Publishing, London.

Periodicals

Campaign (weekly), Haymarket Press Ltd, London.
Conferences & Exhibitions International (monthly), Conference and Exhibition Publications, London.
IPRA Review (quarterly), Longman Group Ltd, Harlow, Essex.
Public Relations (quarterly), Longman Group Ltd, Harlow, Essex.
UK Press Gazette (weekly), Bouverie Publishing Co. Ltd., London.

Books

Corporate Personality, Wally Olins, Design Council, London, 1978.
Dictionary of Marketing, Advertising and Public Relations, Frank Jefkins, Intertext, London, 1983.
Practice of Public Relations, The, W.P. Howard (Ed), Heinemann, London, 1981.
Product Recall Management Guide, Howard Abbott, Product Safety, Kingston-on-Thames, 1983.
Quality Circles, Mike Robbins, Gower Publishing, Aldershot, 1983.
Sponsorship, Victor Head, Woodhead-Faulkner, Cambridge, 1981.

APPENDIX 2:

ADDRESSES OF ORGANISATIONS AND SERVICES

Association For Business Sponsorship of the Arts, 2 Chester Street, London , SW1X 7BB.

British Association of Industrial Editors, 3 Locks Yard, High Street, Sevenoaks, Kent.

CAM Education Foundation, Abford House, 15 Wilton Road, London, SW1V 1NJ.

EIBIS International Ltd, 3 Johnson's Court, Fleet Street, London, EC4A 3EA.

Institute of Public Relations, Gate House, St. John's Square, London EC1M 4DH.

International Association of Business Communicators, 870 Market Street, Suite 928, San Francisco, CA 94102, USA.

International Public Relations Association, Case Postale 126, CH-1211, Geneva 20, Switzerland.

London Chamber of Commerce and Industry, Examinations Bpard, Marlowe House, Station Road, Sidcup, Kent, DA15 7BJ.

Public Relations Consultants Association, 37, Cadogan Street, Sloane Square, London, EC4P 3DP.

Universal News Services, Communication House, Gough Square, London, EC4P 3DP.

GLOSSARY OF ABBREVIATIONS

AA	Advertising Association
ABC	Accredited Business Communicator
ABC	Audit Bureau of Circulations
ABSA	Association for Business Sponsorship of the Arts
ACORN	A classification of Residential Neighbourhoods
AGB	Audits of Great Britain
AIRC	Association of Independent Radio Contractors
AMIPR	Associate Member Institute of Public Relations
AP	Associated Press
ASA	Advertising Standards Authority
AV	Audio visual
BAIE	British Association of Industrial Editors
BARB	Broadcasters Audience Research Board
BCEA	British Exhibition Contractors Association
BIM	British Institute of Management
BMRB	British Market Research Bureau
BOT	Board of Trade
BOTB	British Overseas Trade Board
BRAD	British Rate and Data
BSI	British Standards Institute
BT	British Telecom
CAM	Communication, Advertising and Marketing Education Foundation
Cap	Capital letter
CATV	Cable television
CBI	Confederation of British Industry
CCM	Column centimetre
CEO	Chief executive officer
CERP	Confederation Europeenne des Relations Publiques
CI	Corporate identity
CIO	Chief information officer
COI	Central Office of Information
CRC	Camera-ready copy
DBS	Direct broadcast by satellite
DipCAM	Diploma of the Communication, Advertising and Marketing Education Foundation

Glossary

DipIAA	Diploma of the International Advertising Association
DipM	Diploma of the Institute of Marketing
DoT	Department of Trade
ECGD	Export Credit Guarantee Department
EIBIS	Engineering in Britain Information Service
EMA	Editorial Media Analysis
Extel	Exchange Telegraph
FIPR	Fellow of the Institute of Public Relations
FMCG	Fast-moving consumer good
IAA	International Advertising Association
IABC	International Association of Business Communicators
IBA	Independent Broadcasting Authority
ILR	Independent local radio
IM	Institute of Marketing
IPA	Institute of Practitioners in Advertising
IPR	Institute of Public Relations
IPRA	International Public Relations Association
IT	Information technology
ITV	Independent television
JICNARS	Joint Industry Committee for National Readership Surveys
LBC	London Broadcasting Company
MBAIE	Member of British Association of Industrial Editors
MBO	Management by objectives
MCAM	Member CAM Society. Holders of DipCAM (*see*)
MInstM	Member Institute of Marketing
MIPR	Member Institute of Public Relations
NEC	National Exhibition Centre
NPA	Newspaper Publishers Association
OB	Outside broadcast
OFT	Office of Fair Trading
PA	Press Association
PAO	Public affairs officer
PIMS	Press Information and Mailing Services
PIO	Public information officer
PLC	Product life cycle
PPA	Periodical Publishers Association
PR	Public relations
PRCA	Public Relations Consultants Association
PRSA	Public Relations Association of America
QC	Quality circles
SCCM	Single column centimetre
TGI	Target Group Index
TV-am	Commercial breakfast television
TVR	Television rating
UNS	Universal News Service
UP	United Press
UPITN	United Press International Television News

INDEX

Abbreviations, 75
Abbott, Howard, 81
Account executive, 30, 48
Adenyanju, Banji, 22, 25
Advertising, 5, 10-11, 28-9, 92-3
advocacy, 64
agency, 28-9, 104, 121
co-operative, 65
corporate, 63-4
differences from PR, 118
financial, 65
free, 10-11, 37, 53, 75
generic, 65
issues, 64
professional bodies, 93-4
recruitment, 15
take-over bids, 96
Advertising Standards Authority, 12
Advocacy advertising, 64
After-sales service, 12
Akinyemi, Bankole, Dedication
A la carte advertising agency, 28-9, 104
Allen, Mary, 68, 70
American Notes, 87
Amersham, 96
Annual general meetings, 20, 90
Annual report, 20, 62, 95
Architect's Journal, 94
Argyle Foods, 96
Articles, feature, 75, 93
Arts sponsorship, 67-8, 126
Association For Business Sponsorship of the Arts, 68, 126
Attitude tests, 33
Audio cassettes, 60, 62, 88, 92, 102-3
Authors agents, 51
Awards to journalists, 65, 68
professionals, 68

BAIE Award of Excellence, 113, 114
BAIE Editors Handbook, 114, 117
Banks, 19, 21, 66, 67, 95
BARB, 108, 111
Barker, Lyons, Charles, 102, 103, 104, 105
Barker, Watney and Powell, Charles, 100, 101-2
Barratt, Michael, 17
BBC, 38
BBC, External Services, 22, 56
Radio, 42, 44
Television, 53, 54, 66
Benn's Press Directory, 36, 48, 125
BL, 12, 17, 69, 88
Blue Circle, 68
Bookmakers, 66, 103
Boots, 18
Bosanquet, Christopher, 102
Botulism, 81
BP, 19, 96, 97, 98
Braddon, Russell, 69, 70
Brag sheet, 48
British Airways, 12
British Association of Industrial Editors, 113, 114, 126

Index

British Code of Advertising Practice, 10
British Diabetic Association, 69
British Overseas Trade Board, 22, 23
British Safety Council, 81
British Telecom, 19, 63
Britoil, 96, 97
Broadcasting Gallery, 57
Buckmaster, Maurice, 58, 70
Budgetary control, 30-1, 48
Budgeting, 28-30, 32, 34-35, 38-9, 48, 88
Building societies, 6, 20, 21, 57, 95, 99
Burson-Marsteller, 8, 62, 87, 98-99, 102, 104, 105, 107

Cable and Wireless, 19, 96
Cadbury-Schweppes, 67, 75, 103
CAM Diploma, 116, 122
CAM Society, 116
Campaign, 64, 70, 105, 125
Canon League, 68-9, 103
Canon (UK) Ltd, 68-9, 70, 103
Capital letters, 75
Ceefax, 37
Central Office of Information, 22, 56
Chichester Theatre, 69
China, 19, 67, 69
City editors, journalists, 18, 19, 62, 95, 96, 110
CLEAR, 100-1
Coca-Cola, 22, 66, 103
Codes of Practice,
    BCAP, 10
    IBA, 10
    IPR, 95, 113
    IPRA, 95, 115
    PRCA, 95, 114
    RIBA, 93, 105
Communication Audit, 8, 28, 29, 32, 33, 103, 107
Communication Audit, The, 102-3, 105
Communications, Advertising and Marketing Education Foundation, 112, 113, 116, 126
Community relations, 18, 109-10
Compact cassettes, 60, 62
Company results, 65
COMSAT, 63
Conferences, 61, 63
Conferences & Exhibitions International, 125
Conservative Party, 64
Contact, 125
Contact report, 31
Co-partnership, 88, 90
Coral bookmakers, 66, 103
Corbett, Ronnie, 64
Cornhill Insurance, 40, 66, 103, 106, 108
Corning Glass, 81
Corporate
    advertising, 63-4
    image, 8, 22, 68, 99, 110
    TV commercials, 63
Costs of PR, 26-31
Courtaulds, 12
Covent Garden, 67
Cricket, 40, 66, 106, 108
Crisis
    management, 82-7
    public relations, 4, 8, 79-87, 97
Critical path analysis, 46, 48
Cross-fade, 60
Cruel Poisons Act, 101
CSS Promotions, 67

Daily Express, 36
Daily Mail, 36
Daily Mirror, 57
Daily Star, 36, 57
Daily Telegraph, 37
Dalgety, 19, 96
DC-10, 82
D-Day planning chart, 46-7
Dealer magazines, 21
Dealer relations, 9, 21
Definitions
    publicity, 7
    public relations, 7
Demassification, 38
Dickens, Charles, 87
Discussion group, 40, 107
Dow Chemical Canada, 123-4

Dow's Secret Weapon, 123
Dunk, William P, 20, 25
Dunlop, 69, 75, 103

Economist, The, 20, 70
Edelman & Associates, 104, 105
Edelman, Daniel J, 104
Educational literature, print, 35, 61
Educational sponsorship, 69
Edwards, Michael, 85
EIBIS International, 22, 126
Electronic newspapers, 59, 87
Equity ownership, 88, 90
European Commission, 101
Evaluation, 39-41, 44-6, 102, 106-110
Evening Standard, 44
Evoluon science exhibition, 57
Exhibitions, 55-7, 60, 76
  centres, 55
  mobile, 57
  official opening, 76
  permanent, 57
  portable, 57
  press facilities, 52
  press officer, 56
  private, 35, 57
  public, 55, 76
  trade, 55, 76
Exhibitions, named,
  Broadcasting Gallery, 57
  Evoluon, 57
  Legoland, 57
Expenses, 28, 29
Export PR, 22-3
Extra-Parliamentary action, 100-1
Eyeball-to-eyeball confrontation, 69

Facility visits, 51
Feather, Victor, 51
Feedback, 32-3, 86
Fees, 23, 27, 29, 101
Film, documentary, industrial, 34, 35, 59-60, 63, 65
Film libraries, 60
Financial institutions, 19, 95
Financial PR, 18-19, 95-9, 103-4
Financial PR consultants, 20, 95, 96-7, 103-4
Financial Times, 20, 36, 37, 44, 52, 81, 105, 108, 114
Finger printing, 81
Firestone tyres, 81
Fleet Street contacts, 36
FMCGs, 21, 24, 34, 93
Focus groups, 99
Football, 68-9
Ford, 54, 75, 85
Ford News, 58, 89
Format, 57

Gallup poll, 106
Gas, 2-3, 61
General Motors, 9, 66
Gerstacker, Carl, 123
Gill, Barrie, 67, 70
Gillette, 37, 48, 103
Glenfiddich, 68
Gofton, Ken, 68, 70
Good, Tony, 103
Good Public Relations Group, 103, 104, 105
Good Relations (Corporate Affairs), 119, 124
Goodman, Douglas, 41, 48
Guardian, The, 45, 51
Guinness, 61, 75
Gulliver, Jimmy, 96

Haig whisky, 66
Harveys of Bristol, 18
Haywood and Associates, Roger, 102
Headlines, 75
Hearst, William Randolph, 12
Hedges, Martin, 96, 105
Hidden Persuaders, The, 5, 13
Hill and Knowlton, 94, 95-7, 105
Hollis Press and Public Relations Annual, 114, 117, 125
Honda, 69
Hong Kong, 19, 69, 86, 96
Hospitality, 26, 28, 44, 46, 86
Hot line, 81
Hourly rate, 27, 29, 30

House journals, 4, 16, 28, 35, 47, 57-9, 87, 88, 89-93, 110
  external, 58-9
  internal, 57-8, 87, 88, 89-93
Houston Natural Gas, 98-9

IBA Code of Practice, 10
IBM, 66, 89, 120
ICI, 12, 65
ICL News, 59, 87
Image,
  corporate, 8, 12, 22, 99, 110
  current, 12, 32
  favourable, 11
  mirror, 12
  multiple, 124
  perceived, 12
  studies, 33, 40, 106-7
  wish, 12
Incentive schemes, 88, 92
Independent local radio, 38, 44
India, 12
Indigenised companies, 96
Induction, 17, 60
In-flight magazine, 58
Institute of Marketing, 6
Institute of Public Relations, 23, 70, 100, 112-3, 121, 126
  City and financial group, 96
  Code of Professional Conduct, 95, 126
  Parliamentary Register, 23, 101
Institutional advertising, 63-4
Intelligence system, 33, 96
Intelmet, 63
Inter-Continental Hotels, 63
Internal communications, 88-93
  audit, 16
  downward, 88, 91-3
  sideways, 88, 90-1
  upwards, 88, 89-90
Internal relations, 15-18, 57-8, 87-93
International Association of Business Communicators, 4, 84, 87, 105, 115-6, 126
International Herald Tribune, 20
International Public Relations Association, 95, 115, 126
Interviews, 55, 76-8
Investible Idea, The, 98, 105
Investment analysts, 4, 19, 62, 95
IPRA Review, 105, 115, 117
Isle of Man, 45
Issues advertising, 64
ITN News, 44, 53-4
ITT, 64
ITV, 53, 66

Japanese, 12, 21, 50, 68-9, 85, 90
JICNARS, 108, 111
JICRAR, 108, 111
Job numbers, 31, 48
Job specification, 120
Journalists in PR, 36, 122
Junkets, jollies, 26

Kalamazoo, 90
Kleber, 81
Kleinwort Benson, 19
Kodak Carousel, 60
Korean air disaster, 50, 83
Kotler, Philip, 7, 10, 11, 13
Kransdorff, Arnold, 105
Kraut, G.A., 20, 25

Labour Party, 64, 101
Laker Airways, 82, 85
Laker, Sir Freddie, 82
LBC, 55
Lead poisoning, 100-1
Lego, 57, 85
Letterpress, 71
Levin, Bernard, 5
Lewis Partnership, John, 90
Liberal Party, 15
Lightfoot, Don, Dedication
Lily Industries, 68, 69
Linfood, 96, 97
Lobby correspondents, 51
Lobbying, 23, 100
London Chamber of Commerce and Industry, 116-17, 126
London Marathon, 37, 48
Lowell Offering, The, 87

MacNeill, John, 44
Magicote, 9
Malawi, Dedication
Management by objectives, 14
Manhours, 26-7
Manning, Selvage & Lee Inc, 82
Manuel, Vivian, 83, 86, 105
Marketing, 68, 70
Marketing, attitudes to PR, 6, 24-5, 74
Marketing Education Group, 7
Marketing failures, 9, 10, 24, 41
Marketing research, 6, 33, 39-40, 44, 106-7
Marketing Week, 103, 105
Marks and Spencer, 12, 17, 120
Mars, 37
Martini and Rossi, 67, 68
Martini Royal Photographic Competition, 68
McDougalls cookery book, 24, 61
Mecca bookmakers, 66
Media, 35-6, 88
    coverage, 41-5, 107-9
    created, 35, 38, 88
    macro, 69
    micro, 69
Megarry, Michael, 99, 105
Members of Parliament, 23, 100-2
    employment of, 101
    registers of, 23, 101
Mergers, 17, 92
Mexican Statement, The, 7, 8, 32, 85
Michelin, 15, 61, 62
Midland Bank, 66, 67, 103
Mobil Oil, 67, 68
Monitoring, 33, 106, 108
Monopolies Commission, 23, 96
Moscow, 41
Motivational research, 5
Multi-screen slide presentations, 60
Murdoch, Rupert, 74

National press, 36, 42, 44, 45, 49-50
News, 12
    agencies, 51
    bad, 50-1, 82, 86
    hard, 52
    release, 74-6, 109
News at Ten, 108
News of the World, 74, 108
Newsnight, 54
News release, 74-5
    how to write, 75
    publishable, 74-5
New smoking mixture, 10
New York, 20, 63, 96
Nigeria, Dedication, 22, 25, 67, 69, 96
No comment, 51

Objectives, 14-25, 26-7, 34, 39, 110
Observer, The, 62, 105
Ocean Transport and Trading, 17, 91
Off the record, 72
Offset-litho, 57, 71
Ogilvy and Mather, 64, 70
Olympics, 66
One to one contacts, 69
Open door, 89
Opening paragraph, 74, 75
Opinion polls, 33, 39-40, 160
Opportunities to see, 108
Oracle, 37
Overseas business trips, 61, 62
Overseas PR, 22-3

Packard, Vance, 5, 13
Pamdule, Simon, Dedication
Parliamentary liaison, 23, 100-2
Parliamentary Registers, 23, 101
Persuasion, 6, 9
Pest control, pesticides, 45, 83, 101
Pharmaceutical Society, 94
Philips, 57, 59, 90
Phone-ins, 20, 55
Photo agencies, 51
Photography, 36, 46, 47, 61, 63, 109
Photogravure, 71
Pilkington, 69
Players, 103

Political PR, 23, 100-2
PR in organisational structure, 119
Press,
- conferences, 42, 44, 51
- coverage ratings chart, 108
- cuttings, 14, 28, 37, 93
- kits, 56
- party, 41
- receptions, 46-7, 51, 55, 60, 72, 121
- relations, 36, 37, 74-6, 122
- release, 74-6
- sources of information, 51-2

Press Association, 51
Press, The, 36-7, 71-3
Pressure groups, 100-1
Prestel, 37, 59, 87, 88
Printed literature, 35, 61, 63
Private members bills, 101
Privatisation, 18, 19, 95, 96
Prizes, 54
PRO, attributes of, 122
Product Liability, 81
Product life cycle, 24
Product publicity, 24, 120
Product recall, 24, 65, 81-2, 84
- cost of, 81
- examples, 81

Product Recall Management, 81, 105, 125
Professional awards, 68
Professionalism in PR, 112-17
Professions and PR, 93-5
Profit-sharing schemes, 17, 88, 90
Profits, 16, 17, 19, 88, 90, 96
Progress meeting, 29 30
Propaganda, 5, 6, 64
Properties, 54
Public affairs, 119-20
Public Relations, 25, 48, 70, 113, 114, 115, 117
Public relations consultancies, 4, 16, 23, 28-9, 48, 102-4, 118
- billings, 102, 104
- fees, 23, 27, 29, 101
- retainers, 101

Public Relations Consultants Association, 23, 95, 101, 102, 113-4, 126
Public relations departments, 42, 44, 118-24
- positions in organisation, 119
- qualifications of manager, 121-2
- staff of, 121
- relationship with management, 122

Public Relations Society of America, 112
Public Relations Yearbook, 114, 117, 125
Publicity, 7, 10, 11, 81, 82, 86
Publics, 32, 34-5
Puffery, 11, 75

Quality circles, 88, 90, 105
Quality Circles, 105
Quality of coverage, 102, 109
Queen Elizabeth II, 83
Questionnaire, 39-40, 106, 107

Radio, 38, 42, 44, 45, 54-5, 62, 106
- interviews, 77-8

Rantzen, Esther, 81
Raven, Walter, 96, 97
Recall research, 44
Recruitment, 15
Remington razor, 81
Rentokil, 20, 45-6, 48, 68, 88, 105
- library, 68
- *Roundabout*, 88, 105

Results, evaluating, 39-41, 44-6, 102, 106-10
Retainers, 101
Reuters, 51
Road show, 60
Robins, Mike, 90, 105
Robotics, 85, 88
Rolls-Royce, 50, 80
Rothmans sports annuals, 61, 68
Rowntree-Mackintosh, 18
Royal Commission, 23, 100
Royal Family, 68
Royal Society For The Protection of Birds, 62

Royal Society of British
Architects, 93, 105
Royal Wedding, 37

Saatchi and Saatchi, 12
Safety standards, 17, 81, 85
Sainsburys, 98
Sales contests, 92
Salmon, 81
Sanyo, 68
Satellites, 63, 80, 88
Scottish Television, 73
Scrip issues, 20
Sea Containers, 96
Seminars, 35, 61, 63
Shadow ministers, 23
Share issues, 18, 95, 97-8, 103
prices, 19, 41, 84, 95, 96, 110
Shareholders, 20, 64, 90, 95, 97, 110
Sharp, 68
Shell, 64, 65, 91
Show jumping, 66, 68
Sinclair Research, 88
Sinclair, Sir Clive, 12
Singer Sewing Machines, 58
Single issue pressure groups, 100-1
Six Point PR Planning Model, 15, 25, 32, 48, 49
Slater, Robert, 82, 85, 105
Slides, 60
Smith, Harvey, 68
Social Democratic Party, 15
Sony Umatic, 59
Spalding, Tony, 96
Speak-up schemes, 16, 88, 89
Spillers, 19, 96
Sponsored publications, 61, 68
Sponsorship, 11, 37, 40, 61, 65-9, 103, 106, 107, 108
achievements of, 67
arts, 67
categories of, 67-9
educational, 69
expenditure, 67
local events, 69
results, 106, 108
socialising, 67
sports, 40, 64, 66, 67, 68-9, 103, 106, 108
Sponsorship, 125
Sports sponsorship, 40, 64, 66, 67, 68-9, 103, 106, 108
Stephenson, Don, 123, 124
Stock Exchange, 95, 97, 99
Stone, Derek, 58
Strauss, Levi, 66
Strikes, 85, 90
Striking price, 98
Subject, 74-5
Sumitomo Rubber Industries, 69
Sun, 37, 50, 66, 74, 82, 103, 105
Sunday Concord, 22, 25
Sunday Times, 44
Syndication, 51

Tabloid, 57, 88
Take-overs, 1, 12, 19, 80, 84, 95, 96-7
Tass, 50
Tele-conferencing, 20, 88
Television, 37, 53-4, 64, 66, 76-7, 81, 106
alternative, 37-8
documentaries, 81
interviews, 76-7
studios, 77
three aspects of, 76-7
Test matches, 40, 66, 106, 108
Thalidomide, 80
Thatcher, Margaret, 77
That's Life, 81
Thompson, Clive, 88
Thomson, Lord, 73
Thomson Holidays, 41-5, 48
Thoresen car ferries, 9
TI, 64
Time sheet, 30-1, 48
Times, The, 50, 52, 73
Tobacco, 10, 66
Toffler, Alvin, 38, 48
Trade unions, 16, 90
Travel Agency, 45
Travel trade, 9, 41-5
Travelers Insurance, 58

UK Press Gazette, 65
Universal News Services, 51, 126
Unlisted Securities Market, 103

Venice-Simplon-Orient-Express, 96
VHS, 59, 102
Victoria and Albert Museum, 67, 68
Video, 2, 3, 23, 34, 35, 36, 46-7, 59, 63, 69, 85, 91, 102
  conferencing, 63
  formats, 59
  magazines, 3, 16, 28, 88, 89, 91, 92, 114
Vines, Steve, 87, 105
VM Communications, 83

Wall-charts, 61
Wall Street, 20
Wall Street Journal, 20
Watts, Reginald, 8, 13, 32, 102-3
Web-offset-lithography, 57, 71
West, John, 81
West Nally Group, 37, 48
What Price Public Relations, 102, 105
Whitbread, 66
White papers, 51, 102
Wills, W.D. & H.O., 67, 103
Wilson, Des, 100-1
Wire services, 51
Worker participation, 4, 15, 88, 89-90
Works visits, 21

Zimbabwe, Dedication

Printed in the United States
by Baker & Taylor Publisher Services